CHRISTIAN ENCOUNTERS

SAINT
NICHOLAS

D0905760

CHRISTIAN ENCOUNTERS

SAINT NICHOLAS

JOE WHEELER

THOMAS NELSON
Since 1798

NASHVILLE DALLAS MEXICO CITY RIO DE JANEIRO

Published in Nashville, Tennessee. Thomas Nelson is a trademark of Thomas
Nelson, Inc.

Thomas Nelson, Inc., titles may be purchased in bulk for educational, business,
fund-raising, or sales promotional use. For information, please e-mail
SpecialMarkets@ThomasNelson.com.

Published in association with the literary agency of WordServe Literary Group,
Ltd., 10152 S. Knoll Circle, Highlands Ranch, Colorado 80130.

www.joewheelerbooks.com

Scripture quotations marked NLT are from *Holy Bible*, New Living Translation,
copyright © 1996. Used by permission of Tyndale House Publishers, Inc.,
Wheaton, Illinois 60189. All rights reserved.

Library of Congress Cataloging-in-Publication Data

Wheeler, Joe L., 1936–
 Saint Nicholas / Joe Wheeler.
   p. cm.
 Includes bibliographical references (p.   ).
 ISBN 978-1-59555-115-3
 1. Nicholas, Saint, Bp. of Myra. I. Title.
 BR1720.N46W54 2010
 270.2092—dc22   2010028471

Printed in the United States of America

10 11 12 13 HCI 6 5 4 3 2 1

CONTENTS

INTRODUCTION

Did Saint Nicholas Really Live?

It may seem odd to ask if St. Nicholas really lived, but it is a question that must be asked nevertheless, for if he is but a myth, why on earth should we be including him in this biography series?

Before I spent so many years researching and writing two books on St. Nicholas, this is the issue I took up first. Only when I was convinced beyond a shadow of a doubt that he *did* live, and that his story is certifiably true, was I ready to roll up my sleeves and get to work.

Here is what I have found: there is remarkably little in the way of surviving documents that mention St. Nicholas. This isn't surprising considering that the third-century world St. Nicholas was born into and the fourth-century world of his maturity was a violent one. Even under the *Pax Romana*, life in the vast Roman Empire was never safe.

By the 270s, the Roman emperors were always facing attacks, both from within and without, and it only got worse over time. As Rome began to crumble, it was like a feeding frenzy of ravenous sharks. Towns and cities were burned and ransacked, men and children were killed or sold as slaves, and women were violated and enslaved. The city of Rome became a ghost town, the population plummeting from 1.5 million to a paltry 40,000. Goat herds grazed on its seven hills. It would remain that way for a thousand years. What law and order remained would be in the Byzantine East.

Many succumbed to disease. One plague outbreak (AD 542–594) killed off half the population of Europe. Untold thousands of records were destroyed during the periodic destruction of iconography. These icons (conventional religious images painted on wooden panels) were attacked by those who felt the icons were being worshiped rather than God. A side effect of all this was that most of the church-related records in the East were destroyed. Consequently, it's amazing that any record of St. Nicholas survived, especially when you realize they didn't have any paper to write on: only papyrus, parchment, or vellum, which were incredibly fragile and subject to disintegration and had to be periodically recopied by hand. The Chinese had paper by the second century, but it didn't arrive in Spain until the tenth century, Constantinople until the eleventh, the Italian Peninsula until the twelfth, the Germanic states until the thirteenth, and England until the fourteenth. Mechanized printing was not available in Europe until 1453.

But now let's look at what survived in spite of all that.

We have records showing that after the year 450, more and more clergy chose or were assigned the name Nicholas. Also, there were four early popes named Nicholas. Although there was one minor figure by this name in the New Testament, it's not likely all the clergy chose to call themselves Nicholas by chance. There had to be a prototype, inspiring those who followed to choose his name.

The first surviving Nicholas reference to which we may attribute a measure of validity dates back to the period of AD 510–515. The writer was Theodor, lector of Byzantium. His *Tripartite History* depends entirely on three historians of the fifth century: Socrates, Sozomen, and Theodor. Nicholas's name appears on the tenth line of this AD 510 manuscript in Theodor's list of participants in the famed Council of Nicaea: the 151st attendee is listed as "Nicholas of Myra of Lycia."

In addition to the occasional document mentioning Nicholas and the choice of that name by numerous clergy, we also have buildings with his name. The Eastern Roman emperor Theodosius II (401–450) ordered that a great church be constructed in Myra, and it became known as the Church of St. Nicholas. This would have been no more than two hundred years after Nicholas's death. The last great Roman emperor of the East, Justinian (527–565), codifier of Roman laws and builder of the Hagia Sophia (still one of the wonders of our world), restored another St. Nicholas church. It was rebuilt just outside the summer palace of Blachernes, the primary imperial palace on the Golden Horn. This church was burned by the Slavs and Avars in 626 but was restored and was still standing in 1350. It is inconceivable that a monarch of Justinian's stature would have constructed such a church next to his palace had he any doubts about the tradition of St. Nicholas.

Interestingly enough, the single most significant documentary evidence of St. Nicholas's existence appears in a biography of another bishop Nicholas, Nicholas of Sion. According to historian Jeremy Seal:

> A single reference secures him [Nicholas of Myra]. It dates from the late sixth century, some 250 years after Nicholas's probable death, and occurs in the written life of another saint from the Myra region—another Nicholas, as it happens, who seems to have taken the name as a tribute. St. Nicholas of Sion, sixth century abbot of the eponymous mountain monastery above Myra, will repeatedly tangle with our Nicholas. This other Nicholas, an undoubted narrative distraction, is at once a crucial blessing in that a detail included in his written life serves almost single-handedly to substantiate the life of Nicholas of Myra. St. Nicholas of Sion's life was not only written by a close associate, but was completed shortly after his death. The reference the life contains to our Nicholas in a description of a visit Nicholas of Sion made to Myra—"And going down to the metropolis of Myra, he went off to the martyrium of the glorious Saint Nicholas"—is therefore reliable. Here is his anchor: confirmation that the man who would become Santa once existed.[1]

Michael the Archimandrite (814–842) wrote what is generally considered the earliest reliable account of the life of Nicholas. Both historians D. L. Cann and Charles W. Jones feel he is the one early source they can count on to tell the original unembellished stories. His is the first *biography* of St. Nicholas to survive down to our time intact.

Simeon Metaphrastes's biography was the most widely read and generally accepted text on St. Nicholas. Completed during the second half of the tenth century, it clearly reveals that the people of Lycia deeply venerated the memory of St. Nicholas. In this text we find one of the earliest known references to the church in Myra dedicated to St. Nicholas. It testifies to the annual celebration that took place on his feast day.

Also writing about Nicholas were Peter Damian (d. 1072), cardinal bishop of Ostia; Honorius of Autun (d. 1130); Adam of St-Victor (d. 1192), precentor of the Cathedral of Notre Dame and author of the renowned *Sequences*; Vincent of Beauvais (c. 1194–1264); St. Bonaventure; St. Thomas Aquinas; Dante Alighieri; Jean Gerson; Robert Wace; John the Deacon; Jean Bodel; and James of Voragine, author of the *Golden Legend*.

Historian Will Durant affirms the historicity of St. Nicholas: "St. Nicholas, in the fourth century, modestly filled the episcopal see of Myra in Lycia, never dreaming that he was to be the patron saint of Russia, of thieves and boys and girls, and at last, in his Dutch name as Santa Claus, to enter into the Christmas mythology of half the Christian world."[2]

The *Encyclopedia Britannica* declares that "he was bishop

of Myra in the time of the Emperor Diocletian, was perse-
cuted, tortured, and kept in prison until the more tolerant reign
of Constantine, though Athanasius, who knew all the notable
bishops of the period, never mentions Nicholas. The oldest
monument of the cult of St. Nicholas seems to be the church
of S. S. Priscus and Nicholas built at Constantinople by the
Emperor Justinian."[3]

Clearly, with this evidence before us, we can abandon any
remaining reservations as to whether or not Nicholas was a real
person.

THE AZURE COAST

We begin with St. Paul the apostle because without him there would be no need to write this book. There is a direct tie between St. Nicholas and St. Paul: Paul, who became Christianity's first great missionary and theologian. Paul, who holds a place in Christian history second only to its founder.

Thirteen years after his conversion to Christianity on the road to Damascus, the apostle embarked on his first missionary journey (AD 47–48). It was one of the most significant steps for the early Christians: reaching out beyond Judaism to the Gentiles in the vast Greco-Roman world. During his second missionary journey (AD 49–52), Paul took Christianity into Europe. But it was St. Paul's third missionary journey (AD 52–56) that is most relevant to our story, for gospel writers confirm that one of his stops was at Patara in the ancient province of Lycia. Here, he raised up a company of believers. Two centuries later Nicholas would be born to descendants of those converts. And coincidence of all coincidences, during Paul's year-long voyage in chains to Rome, the vessel he was traveling in stopped at Myra. Thus, with the entire Roman Empire to choose from, the good apostle just "happened" to visit two of the only three cities where St. Nicholas would ever live.[1]

> The landscape [of Turkey's Azure Coast] teems with sophisticated settlements built by the ancient Lycians, a civilization that allied with Troy and crafted perhaps the first federation of cities founded on democratic principles (American founding fathers Alexander Hamilton and James Madison referred to the Lycian model in their papers).
>
> I chose to live along this coast because I feel I have belonged here forever; in my soul, I have always been Lycian. I have walked the Lycian Way, which . . . travels to the many historical sites—ancient rock tombs, Roman amphitheaters and churches that punctuate this striking land. I seek out the villages tucked into the rocky bluffs. . . . I wander weathered hills that offer a bird's eye view of my picturesque hometown and the infinite horizons of the Mediterranean Sea beyond. . . . I visit the millennia-old town of Myra for its beautifully preserved Roman amphitheater and Lycian tombs boldly sculpted from soaring cliff faces. I tour the Church of St. Nicholas, named for its gift-giving fourth-century bishop, who would find reincarnation as Santa Claus.
>
> —Aydin Cukurova, "Land of the Gods"[2]

Indeed, this Azure Coast *is* one of the most beautiful places to be found anywhere in the world. And Patara, about thirty miles west of the Lycian capital, Myra (Demre today), located at the mouth of the Xanthos River, was, back in the third century, a major Lycian city. In its day it was one of the busiest ports in the ancient world.[3] Though relatively small, Lycia has kept its identity for more than 2,500 years. It was part of the vast Persian Empire (550–330 BC), then part of Alexander the Great's Greek Empire for more than four hundred years, and it would remain in the Eastern Roman Empire for almost a thousand years.

In the mid 200s, there lived in Patara a Christian couple: Epiphaneas and Nona, descended from converts St. Paul made here on his third missionary journey. Though their greatest desire was to have a child, many years passed, and still Nona remained barren. Over and over in their prayers, they promised God that if, by a miracle, a boy were born to them, they would dedicate him to God's service.

And then, after thirty long years, during the 270s, the miracle happened; when the midwife announced that their baby was a boy, the parents named him Nicholas (meaning People's Victor).

≈

No more beautiful spot could there have been for a boy to grow up in. The streets were paved with stone and lined with temples, homes, colorful shops, and impressive public buildings, both

Greek and Roman. As the boy Nicholas wandered these streets, he'd have seen—when he looked up—the acropolis, or high city, a place to flee to when danger threatened. Just below the acropolis, another familiar site: the outdoor theater; with twenty-five rows of seats encompassing a 650-meter-long proscenium (the stage of ancient Greek or Roman theaters), it was large enough to accommodate most of the city's inhabitants at once.

Since Lycians were firm believers in education, Nicholas was required to attend grammar school classes. The teacher (or pedagogue) would have taught Nicholas and other students the basics of grammar, arithmetic, and reading, supplemented by selections from Greek classics such as Homer's *Iliad*. In the absence of paper, Homer's *Iliad* and *Odyssey* were kept alive for close to two thousand years by the oral tradition, principally by itinerant orators with prodigious memories, who memorized those epics in their entirety and would recite them in Greek festivals. Nicholas would have practiced his written lessons by either writing with chalk on slate or use wooden tablets containing beeswax writing surfaces. Using the pointed end of a stylus, Nicholas would imprint Greek words and phrases on beeswax; when finished, he'd rub out the impressions with the blunt end of his stylus and be ready to tackle another lesson.

For Epiphaneas and Nona, life would center around the church—not a grand edifice like the Greek temple on the hill, but a small structure with frescoes on the walls and scenes from the Old Testament and the Gospels. Christianity in those days demanded much: Christians were expected to respond to calls for prayers every three hours throughout the day, beginning at sunrise, much as Muslims do today. Because public bath houses were places of occasional indiscreet behavior and because theater performances sometimes bordered on the bawdy and obscene, Christian families tended to keep to themselves most of the time.

But it was not all work, education, and church. For recreation, Nicholas and his friends would play board games, ball games, hide-and-seek, and pretend games fashioned out of wood, bone, clay, or cloth. The family enjoyed visiting neighbors, participating in parties and picnics, and listening to storytelling and music.

But boys being boys, Nicholas would join his friends whenever possible and head down to the waterfront, for there the world came to their door: ships from both the Black Sea and the Great Sea (the Mediterranean); and most exciting of all, great grain ships hauling their life-sustaining cargoes from Egypt to Ostia near Rome would dock here. Since Pataran men always streamed down to the waterfront when a big ship came in, knowing that seamen carried news of the empire with them, Nicholas and his friends would surreptitiously follow. But danger and temptations came from those same seamen—consequently, Nona never breathed easy until she heard Nicholas's step at the door.[4]

THE *DIDACHE*

Sometime during these early years, Nicholas announced his desire to enter the ministry, thanks to the strong encouragement of his parents, his pastor, and a senior priest who offered to mentor him. Greek language and learning provided Nicholas with the requisite foundation in grammar, rhetoric, and philosophy needed for such a course of study. [4]

[5] From Greek records, we learn that Nicholas proved to be an avid student of the Christian faith. He immersed himself in the *Didache*, a document at least as old as the Gospels and letters of the apostles. Of it, historian Cann points out that

> Nicholas and other Christian youths would have learned from it how to live a life inspired by love, how to conduct worship services, and how to live a moral life based on the teachings of Jesus Christ.
>
> The *Didache* is based on Christ's injunction in Matthew 22:37–40, "*'You must love the Lord your God with all your heart, all your soul, and all your mind.' This is the first and greatest commandment. A second is equally important: 'Love your neighbor as yourself.' All the other commandments and all the demands of the prophets are based on these two commandments.*" These teachings were called by contemporaries, "The Way of Life."[5]

Setting the stage for Nicholas's ministry, Cann, referring to the multitudes of people who lived in abject poverty, outlined the need:

> The imperial and provincial governments offered no regular social service programs—people simply had to take care of

themselves or starve. Into that abyss of human need, ignored by provincial and imperial authorities, stepped the Christian communities. Led by bishops, priests, deaconesses, and deacons, the faithful carried out their ministry to the urban poor. The Christian churches of the first four centuries provided hospice care for the sick, as well as support for widows, orphans and the unfortunate. Christians followed the unique Jewish practice of regularizing benevolence and cultivating solidarity within their congregations. From the teachings in the Gospels, the Christians, and young Nicholas with them, cultivated a strong sense of responsibility to care for the souls and bodies of those in need.[6]

No wonder Christianity was turning the world upside down!

2

THE BOY BISHOP

I n the ancient world, the science of medicine being yet in its infancy, most any disease that came along could prove crippling or fatal. Because of this, there was no stopping those periodic plagues that swept across Asia and Europe, killing millions. Sadly, sometime during Nicholas's growing-up years, one such plague bore down on Lycia; by the time it moved on, Patara had been decimated, and Nicholas had lost both parents.

As was true elsewhere in the grief-stricken city, surviving family members stepped in to help. The father superior, who was the boy's uncle, agreed to accept the responsibility of his upbringing, mentoring, and education. As a boy, Nicholas had frequently visited his uncle, and assisted in chanting prayers and participating in religious services; consequently the move from Patara to Xanthos (seven miles upriver) was relatively easy to make. Undoubtedly, his uncle taught him the scriptural, liturgical, and pastoral skills he needed to prepare for Christian priesthood. Besides the *Didache*, Nicholas would have studied, in his native Greek, the Septuagint, the Gospels and Epistles, as well as popular Christian forerunners such as Clement of Rome, Ignatius of Antioch, and Polycarp of Smyrna, who wrote for the early church.[1]

THE DREAM

We do not know exactly when Nicholas became a bishop, just that it was while he was still young. So young that down through history Nicholas is the name most people think of when they hear the terms "Boy Bishop" or "Young Bishop."

One account that has survived to our time, although we can't be positive it is true, is about a dream the young man had. As he was meditating one afternoon in a chapel, Nicholas fell asleep. In his dream he had a vision in which Jesus informed him that a high calling (a significant leadership role) awaited him. Nicholas awoke deeply puzzled. Just what did it all mean?

It wasn't many months before he found out. The aged bishop of Myra died suddenly. Thousands came to the funeral service in the cathedral, and Nicholas joined them in mourning the bishop's passing. The announcement was made that a great Synod would be called during the next few days to elect a successor. It was a heavy responsibility, for the Diocese of Myra was an extremely important one in that part of the empire.

Prayers and deliberations went on for days without any consensus. Who among them had the moral and spiritual stature to fill such shoes?" One night a voice spoke to the most revered bishop in the Synod, commanding him to rise early and station himself at the doors of the cathedral before daybreak and to consecrate as bishop the first man entering the sanctuary who answered to the name Nicholas. Several hours later he shared the injunction with his hastily assembled fellow bishops and urged them to pray that God would bring the right person in at the right time.

Shortly after dawn, the doors were opened for Matins, the early morning prayer service. As the bishop stood in the center aisle, he wondered who might come first.

Nicholas had awakened earlier than usual that morning and was strongly impressed to hurry over to the cathedral. As he walked into the foyer, he cast a shadow on the nave floor. An elderly bishop he didn't recognize abruptly stopped him and asked his name. Respectfully, he answered, "My name is Nicholas, your servant for Jesus Christ's sake." The bishop could not contain his joy and exclaimed in a loud voice that echoed through the empty cathedral, "Thanks be to God, Alleluia!" At this point the members of the Synod (a great number) entered through the cloister door.

Nicholas just stood there stunned: *What could all of this mean?*

The old bishop announced triumphantly, "Here, my brothers, is Nicholas. My dream is true! Let us greet our new bishop." The Synod members began to chant and sing. It was all too much for the young man. He turned to flee, but the verger (a church official) stopped him.

"Nicholas, come forward!" ordered the old bishop.

Still bewildered by it all, Nicholas finally obeyed and was slowly led to the bishop's throne. In the weeks that followed, the news of the new bishop's appointment spread quickly throughout the diocese and beyond. The great day finally arrived, and people came from many miles away to take part in the celebration. They cheered as their friend Nicholas entered the cathedral, dressed in a simple cassock. Several hours later the crowds outside who had been unable to get in saw the massive doors open and Nicholas, bishop of Myra, come forth to bless them and the city. Only now, as he stood there listening to their singing and clapping, as he wore the Golden Mitre and the colorful robes of a bishop with the pallium, and held the gospel book, did his dreams begin to make sense.

THE CRUCIBLE

As time passed and the people of Myra came to know their bishop better, it became increasingly clear that he remained the same Nicholas he had always been: humble, honest, energetic, caring, dedicated, and devoted to his Lord and his flock. His well-known compassion and generosity altered not at all in his new position. When he taught the gospel, people said listening to him was like receiving precious gems. Always he was concerned about the poor, those who were in trouble, those who were mistreated, and the children. His parishioners were quick to note that his giving tended to be done in secret, and many began to emulate him.

Before long, however, a testing time came to the young bishop and his flock. Emperor Galerius, seeing in Christianity the last obstacle to absolute rule, urged his chief, Diocletian, to restore the Roman gods. Diocletian was reluctant to do so, believing there would be a high price to pay for such a step. Galerius waited, certain that Christians would make a mistake he could capitalize on. It happened one day at an imperial sacrifice: a Christian made the sign of the cross to ward off evil demons. Evidently, it worked: the imperial priests were unable to find the marks they hoped to interpret on the sacrificed animals.

In order to find out who had intervened, Diocletian commanded that all who had been in attendance that day had to offer a sacrifice to the gods or be flogged; and that all the soldiers in the army must also conform or lose their positions. When many Christians refused to offer those sacrifices, the stage was set. At Galerius's instigation, in February of 303, the four caesars—Diocletian, Maximian, Constantius (Constantine's father), and Galerius—decreed the destruction of all Christian churches, the burning of all Christian books, the dissolution of all Christian congregations, the confiscation of all property belonging to Christians, and the exclusion of all Christians from public office, and if Christians dared to meet together, they would be put to death. The signal to start this empire-wide attack on the Christian faith was the burning to the ground of the great cathedral at Nicomedia by imperial soldiers.

However Christians were now numerous enough to retaliate. Twice they set fire to Diocletian's palace. Hundreds of Christians were arrested, accused of arson, and tortured. Nicholas—knowing that if he were to go into hiding, his parishioners would suffer all the more because of it—calmly waited for the tread of the imperial soldiery outside the building where he ate and slept. He didn't have long to wait. One night a thunderous knock ordered those inside to open the door immediately—that it was Caesar's will. Nicholas calmly opened it, even though he knew he might never see his people again.

Death would have been easier to take than the fiendish tortures Romans used to break down the resistance of their victims. But somehow, thanks to his faith in the Christ who had endured the anguish of the Cross, Nicholas found the strength to hold out. The pain would mount until flesh and blood could stand no more, and he would mercifully lose consciousness. The next day it would begin all over again.

That September Diocletian ordered the torture of any Christian who refused to worship Roman gods. And he gave orders that soldiers should not wait for Christians to disobey, but should track down every last one.

Maximian carried out the edict mercilessly in Italy. Galerius unleashed a reign of terror throughout the entire East. The roll of the martyrs increased everywhere except in Gaul or Britain, for Constantius alone refused to institute a bloodbath, contenting himself with burning down a few churches. But his realm was the only refuge. The historian Eusebius noted that men were flogged till the flesh hung from their bones, or their flesh was scraped to the bone with shells; salt and vinegar was poured upon the wounds; the flesh was cut off bit by bit and fed to waiting animals; or, bound to crosses, men were eaten piece-meal by starved beasts. Some victims had their fingers pierced with sharp reeds under the nails; some had their eyes gouged out; some were suspended by a hand or a foot; some had mol-ten lead poured down their throats; some were beheaded, or crucified or beaten to death with clubs; some were torn apart by being tied to the momentarily bent branches of trees.

This terrible persecution continued for eight long years. Though thousands recanted under the influence of excruciat-ingly painful torture, many, like Bishop Nicholas, stood firm. Because of this unheard-of willingness to suffer and die for their faith, more and more of the pagan populace began to speak out against the most ferocious oppression in Roman history. In fact, many risked their lives to hide or protect Christians.

By 311, Galerius had had enough. The most widespread persecution in Roman history had failed to force every knee to bow to Caesar and the Roman gods. The people were outraged, the emperor's own guards were sullen about their role in this unrelenting bloodbath, and the Christians continued to choose torture or death rather than worship the emperor. Galerius was dying of a terminal illness. His own wife had turned against his vindictive edict, imploring him to make peace with the all-pow-erful God of the Christians before it was too late. So Galerius finally caved in: he promulgated an edict of toleration, recognized Christianity as a "lawful religion," and contritely asked the Christians to pray for him in return for "our most gentle clemency."

~

What jubilation reigned in the Christian community! In spite of impossible odds, God had brought them through the furnace of persecution. Gradually, dungeon doors began to swing open, releasing those who had stood firm against hell itself. In one of those prisons, one morning a guard descended into the bowels of the earth, unlocked an iron door, and informed a man young in years, but now aged by torture, mistreatment, privation, and separation from the world outside, that he was free.

Few would have recognized this frail man, attired in filthy rags, unkempt, unshaven, unbathed, as the stalwart bishop who had descended into those subterranean regions years before. Years that had seemed endless—without beginning, without end. The guard who had learned to admire the prisoner's inner strength and rock-solid integrity now unlocked the shackles and gently led Nicholas up the many damp steps, through foul air that gradually became pure, up and up and up until the blazing sun and deep blue Mediterranean sky so blinded him he was at first unable to believe this was real. But it *was* real. In the street, he was approached by Christians who asked who he was; when informed, they praised God and assured him that his troubles were over.

Some weeks later a ship sailed into Myra's harbor. Disembarking was a man so changed by all he had endured that at first his own people failed to recognize him. When someone finally exclaimed, "It's our bishop! It's Nicholas himself come back to us! He's not dead after all!" people erupted out of every doorway and engulfed him in a tidal wave of tears, joy, thanksgiving, and love.

When Nicholas returned from prison, inwardly strengthened and seasoned by all that he had endured, the "Boy Bishop" was a boy no longer. Somewhere in that crucible of seemingly unending anguish, he had achieved a level of insight, vision, wisdom, and greatness granted only to those who have been forged in fire. To the people of his time, if anyone deserved to be called a saint, it was he.

So they came to him—all those who needed strength, courage, comfort, even those who were physically sick—and urged him to intercede with the Eternal on their behalf. They did so because there could no longer be any doubt that God and he walked hand in hand. He was famous now, not only among Christians, but among pagans as well.

3

KEPT ALIVE BY STORIES

After the persecution stopped, church properties throughout the empire were finally restored, but it didn't take Nicholas long to discover that the victory won against Caesar did not equate to victory over the Greco-Roman gods. Those gods had been venerated for millennia and showed not the slightest desire to leave. Fiercely did their priests and priestesses hold their ground. Certainly, this was true in Myra's magnificent temple of Artemis. Artemis (known as Diana to Romans), a daughter of Zeus, was viewed as one of the most powerful of all the ancient gods. Artemis was, among other things, the Greek goddess of seafarers, the one sailors prayed to for fair weather and successful sea voyages.

Artemis's temple in Myra was beautiful almost beyond belief, with extensive grounds, complete with many plants chosen for their ability to keep the earth fresh. There was a great inner court, surrounded by columns, altars, and statuary, with a large statue of the goddess. Nicholas had known for a long time that sooner or later he would be forced to battle with Artemis, whom he considered to be leagued with the Dark Power. That war now raged, with no quarter given on either side. In the end, the prayers of Nicholas won out. Simeon Metaphrastes tells the story in these words:

> As soon as the Saint began praying, the altar collapsed, and the statues of idols fell down, like leaves of a tree when a strong wind blows in autumn. The demons who inhabited the place left, but protested to the Saint amidst their tears: "You have been unjust to us. We did you no harm, and yet you send us away from our home. We had made this our home, while these misguided people adored us, and now where can we go?" And the Saint replied, "Go to Hell's fire, which has been lit for you by the devil and his crew." In this manner, all altars in the area were destroyed.

Supposedly, even the demons who ruled there found themselves powerless against Nicholas and his God and fled, shrieking.

THE THREE DOWERLESS DAUGHTERS

The stories of Nicholas's nativity and early years quite likely came later, after the evolution of the myth was already in motion. They helped to build a foundation under the myth by depicting his miraculous birth, his deep spirituality during his earliest years, and how predestined he appeared to be from birth to do great things for God. Even his name was significant—"People's Victor" rather than a victor chosen by a ruler or members of the clergy—for it would be the people who would elevate him to sainthood and keep his memory ever fresh.

Unquestionably, however, it was the story of the "Three Dowerless Daughters" that made St. Nicholas a legend. It had everything going for it: three lovely young women threatened by a fate worse than death, a desperate father, and a wealthy young man who gave away his riches secretly and anonymously. Its authenticity was validated by Michael the Archimandrite.

In those days, men did not marry women who were destitute. Unless the father offered the suitor a dowry, the poor daughter was doomed to be sold as a slave or become a woman of the streets. A neighbor of Nicholas's had three beautiful daughters who were of age. Each had a suitor. Unfortunately, however, the once affluent father lost his fortune. It wasn't hard, in those days of piracy, to lose all one owned in one attack on a trading ship. Now the father faced the darkest days of his life—what should he do? He made it a matter of continual prayer: that God would save his daughters from a fate worse than death. But finally the time came when the decision could be delayed no longer. For the benefit of the other two, the eldest would have to be sold into slavery or forced to become a prostitute; with the money she would bring, the other two could survive awhile longer, and perhaps a modest dowry for one of them could somehow be eked out. The daughters had no say in the matter, for in those days a father's word was law, and women had very few rights. Word spread throughout the community of the family's terrible plight, and the story finally reached young Nicholas.

It didn't take Nicholas long to come up with a plan of action. Knowing that the father would never accept charity, and furthermore being determined to remain anonymous, he decided to act that very night. All his life Nicholas was known for moving into action when the need was greatest. Late that night, approaching the home of the father and his three daughters, Nicholas reached in through an open window and dropped a bag of gold coins on the floor (some maintain that Nicholas climbed up on the roof and dropped the sack of gold down the chimney). The next morning, to the family's joy and astonishment, there was the bag of gold! Weeping in joy and relief, all knelt down to thank God for this unexpected miracle. With this gold, the oldest daughter was able to be dowered and married, with enough left for her father and sisters to live on for some time.

But alas! Before too long, that money was all but gone, and the unthinkable once again had to be faced. Nicholas, who had been secretly monitoring the situation, found out just in time. That night, once again, through the open window went another bag of gold. The next morning there was joy, thanksgiving, tears, and prayers of gratitude to God. With this gold, the second daughter was dowered and married, and there was quite a bit left to live on.

Considerable time passed, and the money held out a long

time. But at last it, too, was gone, and the father informed his youngest that three miracles in a row were just too much to expect. But, bowing to her tears, he kept hoping and praying that somehow God would also save his third daughter. But he strongly suspected that a human being had been God's instrument in saving his two older daughters, and believing that God might still rescue them, determined to stay awake all night so that he might catch the anonymous donor in the act and express his gratitude. Night after night he struggled against sleep as he kept his vigil, but to no avail.

Finally, when delay was no longer possible, in the dead of night in came another sack of gold, this one landing in a stocking hung up to dry by the fireplace. This woke the father, and he chased his fleeing benefactor, shouting all the while, "Stop! Don't run away! I want to talk to you!" With an almost superhuman effort, the father finally caught up with Nicholas. Gasping for breath, he fell to his knees and tried to kiss his benefactor's feet. But Nicholas would have none of it. Reaching down, he raised the man to his feet. Then he told the father that God alone should be thanked for the three bags of gold. Furthermore, he made the father swear a solemn vow that the secret of where the gold came from would never be revealed while Nicholas lived. Reluctantly, the father made that promise. And kept it. Apparently not until after Nicholas's death was the story told (most likely by the daughters). But thanks to that third bag of gold, the youngest daughter was able to be dowered and married.

Although this act was the most famous, many other acts of similar selfless generosity took place. Whenever his identity was discovered, Nicholas exacted a similar promise. A number of these had to do with money; many others involved assistance of a different kind. Whatever help was offered, Nicholas always insisted that no credit or thanks be given to him, but to God only. In this, Nicholas was responding to Christ's repeated injunction that each of us should give in secret, for only in so doing could the giver be blessed. Not surprisingly, in a relatively small community such as Myra, it was not easy to keep this many secrets. Gradually, the people of that region became aware that among them was a selfless human being who went about doing good and directing all praise and gratitude to God.

The post-apostolic church (which dates from the death of the last of those who had seen their Lord in person to the time when Christian congregations began to merge with separate Christian denominations several centuries later) was looking for role models, and Nicholas's selfless giving made him a natural. Through the centuries since then, this has remained the most beloved Nicholas story, transcending ages, transcending time. In fact, many consider it to be the genesis of all gift giving. And the three sacks of gold are represented by the golden balls found on St. Nicholas statues and art.

Two other stories passed down to posterity laid down the foundation for Nicholas's acceptance as a Christian substitute for pagan gods. Helping to control storms made him a shoo-in replacement for Poseidon.

RESCUE THE MARINERS

This particular text was written by Michael the Archimandrite (possibly as early as the eighth century) and was later translated from medieval Greek by the acclaimed Greek scholar Gustav Anrich:

> A ship was driven in a gale in a severe storm and ran aground near shore in the eastern Mediterranean. Caught on the shoals, the ship and its company were in grave danger of destruction as wind and waves battered the ship against the rocks. The captain and crew, having heard of Bishop Nicholas as a holy servant of God, prayed to God for rescue by invoking the name of Nicholas of Myra. The sailors claimed to have received help from Bishop Nicholas himself, who appeared to the crew and encouraged them to reinforce the masts and to free the ship from the rocks.

Bishop Nicholas did not limit himself to advancing the prayers of the sailors and giving them encouragement; he gave them strong and expert help. He pitched in to help the mariners strengthen the lines supporting the masts, and he stood with them when they pushed against the rocks with poles to keep their ship from foundering on the shoals in the violent seas. By the intervention of Saint Nicholas, the crew freed the ship, avoided destruction, and resumed sailing along the coast. The moment the ship pulled away from the shoals, Saint Nicholas vanished as quickly as he had appeared.

The sailors steered their ship to the safety of the harbour of Myra, where they went to the church to give prayers of thanks to God for their rescue. They met numerous clerics, but when they saw Bishop Nicholas, they remembered him as Saint Nicholas who had appeared on their ship. Overwhelmed with awe, the mariners bowed to him and asked how he had heard them praying on their ship during the storm. Bishop Nicholas answered that when people devote their lives to seeking the divine, they are able to gain the faculties of clairvoyance in order to see those in danger and clairaudience to hear their cries for help. Bishop Nicholas then advised the mariners to devote their lives to faithful service to God.[1]

ARTEMIS AND THE BURNING OIL

"Artemis and the Burning Oil" is the second of Michael's stories to incorporate the supernatural. We do not know whether this story preceded or followed the invention of Greek fire by the Byzantine engineer Callinicus in 678. Greek fire would revolutionize warfare almost as much as gunpowder did 650 years later. It was originally packed in clay jars and hurled onto enemy ships, where they would break, then explode. In 941, it saved Constantinople from being captured by an immense invading army of Russians; they jumped into the sea fully armored rather than face it. After that close call, contemporaries began calling Constantinople the "God-guarded City."

This text, too, is Michael the Archimandrite's, translated by Gustav Anrich:

Saint Nicholas, servant of God and celebrated Bishop of Myra, had passed from this world to Heaven. During his life on earth, he had performed many wondrous deeds. Even after his death, he continued to inspire others to holiness. Faithful Christians from across the Empire and from every province therein celebrated and revered him. Pilgrims traveled from all regions to pay homage to Saint Nicholas at his church in Myra. One such group of pilgrims prepared to begin their journey to his holy shrine.

While the pilgrims brought their personal goods to the ship in preparation for their journey, they came to the attention of a malevolent spirit who had been driven from the Temple of Artemis by Saint Nicholas and Christians of his community. Just before the pilgrims set sail for Myra, the evil spirit in the guise of a woman approached them. She handed them a jar containing a liquid and said, "Take this jar as an offering to the shrine of Saint Nicholas on my behalf. I am unable to bring it myself, for I am too ill. When you arrive at the church, I ask that you fill the lamps with this oil."

The pilgrims kindly accepted the jar and set sail for Myra. One night, Saint Nicholas visited one of the pilgrims in a dream and said, "Awaken and throw that jar of evil oil into the sea!" In the morning, the traveler remembered the words of Saint Nicholas and flung the jar into the waves.

Immediately, a flame exploded upon the surface of the

sea, and in the depths the water boiled violently. The pilgrims were terrified at this catastrophe. The ship lurched and tossed in the violent waves. The crew lost control of the ship and struggled helplessly. The ship's company fell into a desperate panic.

Before all was lost, Holy Nicholas quenched the deadly explosion under the sea. When the danger passed and all fears subsided, the pilgrims and the ship's crew safely reached Myra. Everyone gave joyous prayers of thanks to God for sending Saint Nicholas to their rescue.[2]

Each of these stories had its part in contributing to a foundation, a foundation strong enough to anchor a myth that would continue to grow down through the ages. Unquestionably, however, it would be the story of the "Three Dowerless Daughters" that would ensure his immortality among Christians, given that anonymous giving would become his raison d'être.

4

NICHOLAS AND CONSTANTINE

Time plays strange tricks. Who would have been crazy enough to predict that seventeen centuries after their deaths, an obscure bishop from Asia Minor would be better remembered than one of the mightiest rulers in the world?

Flavius Valerius Constantinus, known to history as Constantine, was born in 272, about the same time as Nicholas's birth. Constantine was the illegitimate son of Constantius by his legal concubine Helena, a barmaid from Bythinia who later became a Christian. The young man, like his father, took to soldiering early and proved his valor in wars with Egypt and Persia. When Constantius died at York in 306, his soldiers acclaimed his son Constantine as Caesar.

But with six caesars claiming supremacy at once, the Roman Empire spiraled into chaos. Six years later Constantine cornered one of them, Maxentius, at the Tiber. According to Eusebius of Caesarea (an historian and confidant of Constantine), on the afternoon before this pivotal battle, Constantine had a vision: he saw a flaming cross in the sky, along with three Greek words, *en toutoi nika* ("in this sign conquer"). That night Constantine was commanded in a dream to have his soldiers make a flag with a particular design on it: an *X* with a line through it and curled around the top—the symbol of Christ. When Constantine awoke the next morning, he immediately ordered the creation of a new standard, thereafter known as the *labarum*. Under the banner, Constantine defeated Maxentius, making him master of the western half of the empire. It took ten more years before Licinius, another Caesar, was defeated in the East.

During those seventeen long, bloody years leading up to the moment that he became the ruler of the Roman Empire, Constantine had more than enough time to decide what he'd do if he became emperor. Finally, he concluded that the city of Rome was too corrupt to be worth saving. Thus, immediately after his final battle at Chrysopolis against Licinius, he implemented his momentous decision to move the capital of the empire from the Tiber to the Golden Horn.

If you look at today's map, it's hard to understand Constantine's reasoning. But if you open a Bible to maps that detail the missionary journeys of the apostle Paul, you'll notice that the eastern Mediterranean was then the hub of early Christianity. By the time of St. Nicholas and Constantine, almost three centuries later, it was even more so. Throughout

Asia Minor, a minimum of 25 percent of the population professed Christianity. Powerful bishops ruled great sees such as Alexandria, Carthage, Jerusalem, Hippo, Caesarea, Damascus, Ephesus, Athens, and Byzantium.

Other Christian centers were Thessalonica, Berea, Corinth, Philippi, Thyatira, Pergamum, Miletus, Nicomedia, Colosse, Myra, Lystra, Philadelphia, Sardis, Laodecea, Memphis, Babylon, Capernaum, Neopolis, Gaza, Tyre, Sidon, Heliopolis, Petra, Thebes, Adrianopolis, Seleucia, and Derbe. These cities just happened to be the center of St. Nicholas's world.

Byzantium was already almost a thousand years old when Constantine decided to build "New Rome" there. The emperor chose wisely, for no site on earth could have surpassed it, situated as it was on the crossroads of the world, the place where Europe and Asia meet, where the West ends and the East begins.

In November of 324, Constantine the Great led a small army of aides, engineers, priests, and others from the harbor of Byzantium out across the nearby hills. As they progressed, the foundation positions of the proposed new capital were duly marked. When some questioned why the site was so vast, Constantine answered, "I shall advance till He, the invisible God who marches before me, thinks proper to stop."

Afterward, he summoned thousands of workmen to build the great city. And he issued orders that the finest and most acclaimed art and the most important Christian relics in the empire should be requisitioned and sent to the new capital. Great walls were constructed, as were palaces, homes, administrative buildings, squares, boulevards, and fountains. A magnificent hippodrome for the people's games that seated seventy thousand was also constructed. The city was dedicated on May 11, 330. Within seven years, fifty thousand people had moved in; by AD 400, a hundred thousand; and by AD 500, almost a million. For over a thousand years it would remain the richest, most beautiful, and most civilized city in the world.[1]

Casting about for ways to validate his decision to leave the legendary City of Seven Hills, Rome, and to capitalize on his political marriage with Christianity, Constantine came up with an inspired solution: plunder the ancient world of its greatest artifacts and delegate to his Christian mother, Helena, the responsibility for making his namesake city the pilgrim capital of the empire. She used her imperial powers so effectively that she requisitioned "the prize pieces from the faith's defining drama, Christ's Passion": "a portion of the True Cross, pieces of the two crosses that flanked it, the lance that pierced Christ's side, the sponge used to moisten His dying lips with vinegar and myrrh, the Crown of Thorns, the table used for the Last Supper," the "column of flagellation" where Christ was whipped, and the stone of unction on which his corpse was embalmed.[2]

Not content with all that, Constantinople's chief officials sent teams out across the Near East to find even more, thus adding Christ's infant swaddling clothes; the mortal relics of the three Magi, as well as the vessels that contained the gifts of gold, frankincense, and myrrh; the Virgin Mary's veil and girdle; the head of John the Baptist; the bones of Andrew (taken from Greece) and Luke and Timothy (from Ephesus). It was even said that they were able to track down the twelve baskets Christ fed the five thousand from, and the ax with which Noah built the ark!

Although one can't help wondering about the origin and validity of these relics, when we consider that it would have been no more difficult for Helena to have requisitioned— on firsthand expeditions to Palestine—these precious Jesus Christ–related artifacts than it would be for us to assemble a collection of colonial artifacts in America today (the time frame being roughly equal), it *is* possible that some surviving artifacts—such as the much-debated Shroud of Turin—might be authentic.

Besides all of this, Constantinople later harbored hundreds of monasteries, over a dozen palaces, magnificent moated walls, and the incomparable wonder of the world, the basilica of St. Sophia.[3]

As time passed, and he consolidated his power, he began to favor the Christians more and more, and gave their leaders civil power to go along with their religious power. But what he hadn't counted on was the fallout from terminating the periodic Christian persecutions. As long as they were suffering or dying for their faith, the church remained pure, but when they became dominant politically, the church quickly broke up into snarling sects, each determined to injure or destroy the others.

Constantine was appalled when these great cracks in the

Christian community were brought to his attention—especially the worst crack of all: the heresy preached by a tall, thin melancholic mystic from Alexandria named Arius. Arius maintained that Christ was not a coequal with God, but merely the first and highest of all created beings. Congregation after congregation split right down the middle on the issue, and soon the entire eastern Roman Empire was aflame with it. Even though Constantine was not a theologian, he was astute enough to realize that if Christ was not perceived to be God, Christianity would disintegrate, with a devastating impact on the stability of the empire.

THE COUNCIL OF NICAEA

In 325, Constantine summoned a great conclave from all across the empire to meet in Nicaea near his summer palace in Bythinia. Perhaps never before or since, with the single exception of the 1551 Diet of Worms, has there been such a magnificent assemblage of prelates.

The morning of that May 20 was one the participants never forgot: the deep blue sky of Bythinia, the grandeur of the sprawling palace and its great hall, the sight of famous bishops walking into the hall in all their episcopal glory. Here and there were figures who towered over their age: personages such as the bishop of Alexandria, the bishop of Antioch, the bishop of Jerusalem, the bishop of Nicomedia (Eusebius), the bishop of Cordova, and the bishop of Caesarea (another Eusebius).

Also attending were the next generation of bishops, including Athanasius, destined to become bishop of Alexandria.

The opulence of the magnificent palace must have seemed almost surreal to Nicholas and his fellow bishops, so recently tortured and entombed in dungeons. What must it have been like to have been Nicholas, sitting there with his fellow bishops? Fortunately, someone did take notes, Eusebius of Caesarea, for his landmark book, *Life of Constantine III*.

According to Eusebius, the council to resolve the dispute convened in the largest hall within the palace. Tiered seating lined the walls. The clerics entered and took their assigned seats. When the bishops and other invitees to the council had seated themselves, they grew quiet in anticipation of the emperor's entrance. The emperor's inner circle of friends entered the hall one by one and formed two lines to either side. A signal alerted the approach of the emperor, and everyone stood up. Emperor Constantine entered the hall between rows of his friends. He was adorned like a messenger from heaven—from his light-colored mantle to the sheen of his purple robe, and the rainbow sparkles of light reflected in the gold and gems that studded his garments—and his physical appearance was matched by his imperial bearing. When Constantine had advanced to the end of the tiers of seats to a small gilded chair, he first nodded to the bishops, who returned his acknowledgment, and then sat down, followed by the bishops.

The bishop seated immediately at Constantine's right side stood to deliver a poetical speech, offering a hymn of gratitude to God for their beloved emperor. In the silence that followed, all eyes rested on the emperor. Constantine regarded those assembled before him, and then began to speak in Latin with a Greek interpreter.

It must have been an incredible sight to behold: the emperor himself not only moderating but participating in discussions. All around the great room, members of the stern-faced imperial guard stood, swords at the ready; attendants bustled back and forth, and 159 bishops in their finery sat on one side and 159 on the other. The debate would rage for sixty-six days, from May 20 to July 25.

Constantine was unbelievably patient: when bishop after bishop would attack the position of another, always he would steer the combatants toward consensus. All the major schism issues were addressed, even those espousing monasticism and the self-righteous positions of the Donatists, who postulated that only the pure could be trusted to govern, and conveniently they were the only ones who maintained that purity.

But the powder keg in the room had to be Arius himself, the real reason Constantine had sidelined all the other pressing issues of the empire in order to call the conclave together. Arius was given plenty of time to articulate his views. But the opposition was well prepared. Clever questioning forced Arius to admit that if Christ were but a created creature, what was there to prevent him from veering out of virtue into vice? Pugnacious and astute Archdeacon Athanasius of Alexander, a brilliant theologian and debater, pointed out that if Christ and the Holy Spirit were not one with the Father, then polytheism would be a given.

According to the Athenian monk Damaskinos, this is what took place as Arius was presenting his case:

> The emperor was sitting on his throne, flanked by 159 bishops to his left and 159 to his right. Arian was presenting his views with great vigor and detail. As Saint Nicholas observed the scene, the bishops listened to Arius in complete silence and without interrupting this discourse. Outraged, and prompted by his saintly vigor, he left his seat and walked up to Arius, faced him squarely and slapped his face.

Naturally, the assembly was shocked; Arius's supporters lost no time in appealing directly to the emperor, reminding him that it was not only unlawful for anyone to have the temerity to attack another in his presence, but the legal penalty was to have the offending hand cut off.

When Constantine referred the matter to the bishops, after conferring they advised the emperor to permit them to strip Bishop Nicholas of his clerical garments, remove him from their midst, and place him under guard. Constantine accepted their counsel in all respects. What supposedly followed became fodder for another legend: during the night, Nicholas was visited by Jesus and His mother, Mary, who freed him from his shackles, restored his clerical garments to him, and presented him with a volume of the Holy Scriptures.

The next morning, when the jailer came in and saw the bishop unshackled and re-arrayed in all his vestments, he rushed out to tell his superior about the miracle. It took no time at all before the news got back to the emperor and the conclave. Constantine asked that Nicholas be freed, and then asked for his forgiveness personally.[4]

It appears probable that the original account has been embellished. Quite possibly, the good bishop may have lost his composure and attacked Arius personally; however, the heavenly visitation section quite likely was added later for effect. In all probability, the fact that Nicholas's impulsive act weighed in on the emperor's side rather than on Arius's saved him. Secretly, Constantine may have enjoyed it, yet felt that the firebrand deserved a lesson for forgetting in whose presence he was sitting.

The bishops had already discovered Constantine to be surprisingly knowledgeable about doctrine, especially when he suggested that Eusebius (the recording secretary) insert into the transcript "of one substance with the Father" to describe the nature of the Son, in spite of the fact that in 268 the Council of Antioch had condemned the phrase.

In the end, most of the bishops, not being trained theologians, would most likely have arrived at no consensus on what to do about Arius had it not been for Constantine's firm hand on deliberations. But Constantine, fully realizing the stakes, not only for the church, but the empire, kept their feet to the fire until they grudgingly hammered into preliminary shape the document ever after known as the Nicene Creed:

We believe in one God, the Father Almighty, maker of all things visible or invisible, and in one Lord Jesus Christ, the Son of God, begotten . . . not made, being of one essence (homoousion) with the Father . . . who for us men and our salvation came down and was made flesh, was made man, suffered, rose again the third day, ascended into heaven, and comes to judge the quick and the dead.

Only five bishops were denounced initially by the Council. Three of them later backed down rather than be exiled. At the end, only two remained, including the "unrepentant Arius." The emperor made his position clear by exiling them and issuing an edict that ordered all Arian books to be burned and the concealment of his books a crime punishable by death. The Nicene Creed would eventually lead to the defeat of Arianism and the victory of Orthodox Trinitarianism.

Then, with a giant sigh of relief, Constantine honored the bishops with a state dinner in the palace. According to Eusebius, that event almost defied description: Palace guards stood with swords drawn in formation at the doors. The guests passed the guards and entered the rooms of the imperial household. They reclined at tables on couches, some with Constantine and others to either side. The emperor's hospitality was outstanding, and he offered gifts to each of his guests.[5]

≈

The Constantine-related Nicholas stories are fascinating for a number of reasons, especially for what they imply about the people's relationship to their emperor and how contemporaries viewed the already almost mythical bishop.

THE THREE GENERALS

Undoubtedly this is the longest, and oldest, of all the St. Nicholas stories. Note the repetition of threes; St. Nicholas mythology is replete with triplets (symbolic of his earnest defense of the Trinity).

Constantine was constantly having to put down rebellions across the vast empire. The particular revolt in this story occurred in Phrygia, southeast of Byzantium (Constantinople). Constantine sent three of his most trusted generals, Ursos, Nepotianos, and Herpylion, to quell the outbreak, but storms forced the expeditionary forces to seek refuge in Port Andriaki and Myra. With time on their hands, arguments between the soldiers and tradesmen led to fighting, looting, and general destruction.

The generals, relaxing back at the harbor, were blissfully unaware of the commotion farther inland.

Unaware, that is, until Bishop Nicholas burst into their midst, demanding to know under what authority their soldiers were permitted to loot peaceful villages.

"Looting? Where? How could it have happened?"

The bishop was stern. "*You* are to blame, for you have permitted your soldiers to go on this rampage."

The generals rushed to Myra's public market. Upset by

their troops' lack of discipline, they shouted to restore order and had some of them flogged. While the townspeople and the soldiers joined forces to repair the damage, Nicholas invited the three generals to join him for refreshments in the Cathedral of Myra. Then, after advising and blessing them, the group left the cathedral and began walking down to their ships.

≈

The second part of the story took place before all the soldiers had returned to their ships. Only minutes after leaving the cathedral with the princely generals, the bishop heard the sound of weeping. The cause was not difficult to find. At that time, the provincial prefect was a man named Eustathios, widely known to be so corrupt that he was willing to sentence to death and execute innocent people if a bribe was high enough. Now, because of him, three innocent people were about to be beheaded in the center of town.

Clearly, there was not a moment to be lost! Nicholas and the three generals reached the scene of the execution just in time. Nicholas rushed up to the executioner and ripped the sword out of his hand. Angry and exhausted, he untied the ropes that bound the victims and set them free. News of the event spread like wildfire through Myra and Andriaki, and people streamed toward the execution square from all directions.

Alarmed by all the commotion, Prefect Eustathios mounted his horse and rode toward the square. Seeing him, the bishop stopped his horse and castigated him for his corrupt acts; then he turned to the three generals and announced that he was going to personally inform the emperor of his prefect's unworthiness. At that, Eustathios was "seized by fear" and fell on his knees to beg forgiveness and confess the error of his ways. Forgiveness was granted, and all returned from whence they had come.

Following this, the three generals led their troops into Phrygia, successfully crushed the revolt, and returned in triumph to Constantinople. Highly pleased, the emperor rewarded them with rich gifts and promoted them to even higher rank.

≈

The third part of the story has to do with the aftermath of the mission to subdue the revolt. The adulation showered on the three victors aroused so much envy among their rivals that some of them resorted to lying to Evlavios, the imperial chancellor. Some military leaders who wanted to rule Phrygia themselves told the chancellor that instead of subduing the revolt, the generals had enriched themselves and encouraged their own soldiers to join the revolt. And just to make sure Evlavios was firmly in their camp, the rivals bribed him with a large sum of money.

Evlavios imprisoned the generals, but he was no fool. He sent couriers into Phrygia to find out whether or not the story was true. As time passed, the rivals became more and more apprehensive. So much so that they gave the chancellor more and more gold, urging him to put the generals to death quickly lest the jail be raided and the generals set free.

Evlavios was caught in his own mess: he neither wished

to be personally responsible for the death of the three generals nor to repay any of the bribe money. So he went to the emperor and told him that the three generals were guilty of treason and were now awaiting their fate in prison. "What should be done with them?"

All his life, Constantine was known for his quick decisions. Assuming that his chancellor's reports were correct, he ordered the accused to be executed the following day.

The generals were stunned, for they considered themselves to be among the emperor's most faithful and trusted commanders. And now, suddenly, they were condemned to death without official accusation or explanation. It made no sense. "How did we offend either God or emperor," they wondered, "that we should be treated this way?"

It was Nepotianos who, realizing that no human power could save them, finally thought of St. Nicholas. He urged his associates to plead with God and St. Nicholas to save them, just as the bishop had saved the lives of the three innocent men in Myra. So they knelt down and prayed all night.

Shortly before dawn, the emperor dreamed that a stately figure stood before him and said, "Arise, Emperor—rise quickly! You must free three innocent men whom you have condemned to death! If you do not free them, God will involve you in a war that will cause your death."

Constantine, still not sure that this wasn't just a dream, said, "Who are *you* to threaten me, and how did you manage to break into the palace in the middle of the night?"

Nicholas said, "I am bishop of Myra, and God has sent me to tell you that those three men must be freed without delay!"

The chancellor was also visited in his dreams. In his case, the apparition spoke with all the subtlety of an Old Testament prophet: "Evlavios, you who appear to have lost your mind, tell me why you so lowered yourself and your high office that you permitted yourself to be bribed! Furthermore, why have you permitted such a thing to happen to three innocent men? Free them immediately, or I'll ask God to take your life!"

Evlavios guiltily asked the visitor who he was. The bishop identified himself, after which the chancellor awoke, confused, apprehensive, and in a quandary. Then there was a loud knock on his door, and an imperial messenger rushed in and ordered, "Get dressed immediately—and hurry! The emperor has summoned you!"

The chancellor did so and was soon with the emperor. The two then compared dreams. It was decided to immediately summon the generals to the palace.

When they arrived, haggard from worry and lack of sleep, Constantine demanded that they tell him what magic they had used on him and the chancellor to awaken them in the middle of the night with the same dream.

The generals looked at one another apprehensively. Filled with fear, they were incapable of speech. Finally, the emperor took mercy on them and said in a more kindly manner, "Go ahead; you can answer without being afraid. I'm your friend as well as emperor."

Finally, the whole story came out, and Constantine was silent for a time, pondering what had taken place and what measures should be taken to rectify things. He then turned to the three and pronounced them free. He had with him a gold-covered Bible manuscript, a gold incense vessel, and two gold-plated candlesticks. These they must take to St. Nicholas and tell him that the emperor had obeyed him, but please "don't threaten him anymore!"

The three generals then gave away all their rich possessions, became monks, and, as the emperor had ordered, presented his gifts to Bishop Nicholas, bowed low to the ground, and offered their heartfelt gratitude. But the bishop broke in kindly, raised them to their feet, and told them that no gratitude was due him, but rather to the God who had so miraculously saved them.[6]

THE GREAT FAMINE

In Voragine's *Golden Legend*, we find another Constantine-related Nicholas story:

> There was a great famine in the region where Bishop Nicholas lived, so that finally there was no food left for anyone to eat. Now the man of God learned that some merchant ships loaded with corn were moored in the port harbor. Immediately, the bishop set out for the port area. There he asked the sailors and their leaders to come to the aid of the

starving city by each sharing a little: say a hundred measures of corn from each vessel. The sailors responded that they really wished they could do just that, but the grain had been carefully measured and weighed in Alexandria; if any were missing when they arrived to unload at the imperial granaries, their lives might be forfeit. The saint responded, "Do as I tell you, and I promise, through the power of God, that there will not be any grain missing when you reach the emperor's granaries." Somewhat fearfully, they acceded to his request. Sure enough, arriving at the capital, the emperor's steward found that not a measure of corn was missing. They told everyone of this miracle, and praised and glorified God and his servant Nicholas. As for the corn they had given him, Nicholas distributed it to everyone according to their need, and miraculously provided not only enough food for two whole years, but grain for sowing as well.

THE CHARTER

According to this story, Nicholas journeyed to Constantinople (a little over five hundred miles by land, but probably twice that far by sea) to see the emperor about granting a charter of liberties to the citizens of Myra. After receiving it, St. Nicholas heaved it into the sea. (We never learn how or where this act takes place.) Apparently, word got back to Constantine about the latest act by that firebrand bishop of Myra. Constantine sent guards to St. Nicholas and demanded an accounting.

Nicholas calmly told them the Charter had already been delivered to the citizens of Myra. Not believing that tale for a minute, Constantine sent a delegation to Myra to find out (by ship, this round trip would probably have taken a number of weeks). The delegation discovered that the charter had washed up on the Myra shore the very day it had been signed in the capital.

THE GOLD PIECE

A pauper grieved because St. Nicholas Day was soon to come, and he was so poor he had nothing to offer him. While asleep, he dreamed that a venerable old man pulled out a gold piece. On awakening, there before him was the piece of gold! The story of this miracle quickly spread, even reaching the ears of the emperor, who summoned the pauper to the palace and exchanged the pauper's one miraculous gold piece for twenty-four others. These the pauper joyfully gave to St. Nicholas.

POWER OVER FIRE

St. Nicholas was perceived as one to turn to where fire danger was concerned. In this particular account, an irresponsible mother living in Patara very badly wanted to rush over to the cathedral so that she could see the installation of Nicholas as bishop. Unfortunately, she had a baby and could not take it along. As she was bathing her baby in a tub of hot water placed over a fire, she decided to leave the baby there and go to the service anyway. After the service, she returned only to find that the water in the tub was now boiling, but her baby had been miraculously preserved from death by St. Nicholas, and was happily playing away, oblivious to the temperature.

≈

Notice that in "The Great Famine," Nicholas is portrayed as one for whom God works miracles. From this story the earliest iconographic symbol of St. Nicholas was born: three loaves of bread. "Saint Nicholas loaves" became such a standard symbol that, as late as the seventeenth century, Mediterranean sailors refused to leave harbor without such loaves to throw overboard and calm the waters in case they encountered a storm.

≈

Constantine lived only twelve more years after the Council of Nicaea. On Easter of 337, there was an empire-wide celebration of the thirtieth anniversary of his becoming Caesar. But even as the celebrations continued, the emperor knew the sands of his life were running out. As the end drew near, he finally took the long-delayed step: he called for a priest to administer the sacrament of baptism to him. He had many sins to account for, including the executions of a wife, son, and nephew. But even so, he was a far better man than most rulers of his time.

The good bishop would outlive his liege-lord by only six

years. By this time, Nicholas's fame was already radiating in waves out of his native Lycia into the great East. It was his good fortune to be born in the right place at the right time: the end of the old Roman Empire and the beginning of the Byzantine Empire; at the end of the post-apostolic church and the beginning of the Orthodox and Catholic churches; at the end of the pagan world and the beginning of the Christian world. During his brief life span, he would be a victim of the last great persecution of the Christians; he would see the rise of Donatism and the beginning of its long decline. He would experience the earliest stage of monasticism. And he would be one of the fiercest gladiators in the most pivotal war the Christian church has ever fought: Trinitarianism versus Arianism.

As we shall see, Nicholas will go on to become all things to all people, as each age reinvents him. The patron saint of practically everybody. A man who will refuse to stay dead. A man who will have immortality thrust upon him, whether he'd have wanted it or not. And, perhaps strangest of all, a man who, like the proverbial Wandering Jew, will wander through the centuries playing many parts in the great drama between the forces of Good and Evil.

According to Voragine's *Golden Legend*, "when the Lord decided to take Nicholas to Him, the Saint prayed that he might send him his angels. With head still bowed in prayer, he saw them approaching. He recited the Psalm '*In te Domine sperari*' [In Thee, O Lord, have I trusted (Psalm 30 and 31)], and when he reached the words '*In manus tuas Domine commendo spiritum meum'* [Into thy hands, O Lord, I commend my spirit (v. 5)], he breathed his last, and at his passing, the heavenly choirs were heard. This was in the year of our Lord 343." And the mists of Myra closed in around him.[7]

5

BYZANTINE AUTUMN

The good bishop was dead
When he took his last breath,
Some say.
I say he just
Began to live
That day.

I can't think of a more telling way to begin the rest of St. Nicholas's story than to rephrase one of Emily Dickinson's poems. For Nicholas was indeed anything but dead.

Lending support to the continuing awareness and daily involvement in our lives by St. Nicholas in the eyes of many Nicholas scholars is the irrefutable and otherwise inexplicable presence the good saint has managed to orchestrate down through the ages. Some have noted that it's almost eerie how he appears to be the ultimate pragmatist or opportunist: always aware of just the right moment to move on—and where to go. How else could we explain one of the most fascinating and longest-lasting soap operas in earth's history? The plot is so improbable an astute writer of fiction would never even attempt to chronicle it.

Yet . . . it has all happened. And here is the story.

THE EMPIRE SPLITS

Constantine's successors shared his great dream of making Constantinople—the New Byzantium, the New Rome—the greatest city in the world. The Byzantine Empire's Golden Age would be the reign of Justinian (527–565) and his beautiful wife, Theodora. Justinian could afford to breathe easy, for forty miles of great walls, some two hundred feet thick, stretching from the Sea of Marmara to the Black Sea, now made Constantinople close to impregnable. Well over a million people lived within those walls. Justinian was fortunate to have Belisarius as his general, one of the greatest military leaders this world has ever known. With him at the helm, the empire vastly expanded: all of northern Africa was recaptured from the Vandals, as was southern Spain; the Ostrogoths were defeated in Italy as well. Justinian is also remembered for his revision of the legal system, which became known as the Code of Justinian. It lasted for almost a thousand years in the Byzantine Empire and lives on in modern jurisprudence throughout the world. Justinian is also responsible for the construction of one of the most beautiful buildings ever built, the Hagia Sophia. Ten thousand workmen were needed, and an astronomical 320,000 pounds of gold ($320,000,000 at today's prices) was spent, which just about drained the imperial treasury. On December 26, 537, the emperor and patriarch of Constantinople led the inaugural procession into the great cathedral. Filled with awe and joy, Justinian lifted his hands and cried out, "Glory be to God who has thought me worthy to accomplish so great a work! O Solomon! I have vanquished you!"[1]

Justinian's reign was the peak. Never again would Constantinople rule over so vast an area. After Justinian died, the empire contracted again. St. Nicholas was celebrated as the great city's patron saint until the iconoclastic purges almost tore Christianity apart, and then again when iconography was restored.

In 972, Germany's emperor Otto II married the Byzantine princess Theophano. She introduced St. Nicholas to the imperial court there. But an even more significant marriage (in terms of impact on the culture) was that of Theophano's cousin, Byzantine princess Anna, who married Vladimir, Grand Duke of Kiev (972–1015). Vladimir supposedly gave up five wives and eight hundred concubines when he married her. Then Vladimir ordered the entire population of Kiev to walk into the Dnieper River and be baptized en masse. As a result, all Russia eventually became Orthodox. Since Nicholas was revered by more Russians than was any other saint, he became the patron saint of all Russia.

THE ARABIAN WHIRLWIND

Far to the east, in 570, a major player in the Nicholas story, Mohammed, was born into a poor family in the desert. This unlettered child would grow up to write one of the world's most significant books, the Koran. Since he was a descendant of Abraham and Hagar, Mohammed felt himself to be heir to both Jewish and Christian traditions and thought. Both were incorporated into the Koran. The new faith spread like fire in a tinder-dry forest. The Arabians, led by great tacticians and mounted on some of the world's fastest horses, then set out to conquer the Mediterranean world. Saracen fleets attacked by sea as horsemen attacked by land. "There is no god but Allah, and Mohammed is His Prophet," rang out everywhere, and cities that had been Christian since apostolic times now turned Muslim. Unlike the Byzantines and other Christian rulers, the Arabs evidenced toleration to all, regardless of their faiths, and this fact not only made Arabian victories easier but also made their reign more permanent. Almost overnight, the great Christian East became the great Muslim East; the Mediterranean an Arab lake, and the powerful sees of Alexandria, Antioch, and Jerusalem were no more.

So here we have the eastern Roman Empire, shrunken again, but amazingly, still alive. The year 1000 arrives, and the world does not come to an end; neither does Christ return. In 1036, the Normans invaded Italy. The bravest and wiliest of all the Norse leaders was Robert Guiscard, who had pretensions of making himself the mightiest monarch in Europe. He almost succeeded, defeating the Byzantines twice. In 1071, he conquered Bari, on Italy's south coast.

THE STORIES CONTINUE

Thanks to the story of the three dowerless sisters, Christians were now honoring St. Nicholas by imitation, giving presents to those who were in need. It is very likely that the later practice of hanging up stockings at Christmas stems from the stocking-like sacks the gold was in and the fact that the third sack landed in or on a stocking hung up to dry by the fireplace. The story also reminded Christians of Christ's injunction to give secretly (Matt. 6:3).

Members of the post-apostolic church took literally Christ's promise in John 14:12–13 (NLT): "The truth is, anyone who believes in me will do the same works I have done, and even greater works, because I am going to be with the Father. You can ask for anything in my name, and I will do it." Because of such promises, they believed that St. Nicholas would intercede for them if they only asked him.

After St. Nicholas's death, the myth really began to grow. So much larger than life had he been perceived that it seemed only natural to his contemporaries that God would have called the good bishop to heaven after his death—therefore, many assumed they now had an advocate they knew and trusted to intercede for them. Life was fragile, with almost any wound or disease likely to prove fatal. And the Mediterranean was so dangerous weather-wise that women never knew from day to day whether their menfolks' fishing boats would return at day's end. And so often were these prayers invoking the good bishop's name followed by the desired results that their faith in such intercession exponentially increased. As his stature in Christendom grew, so did the number of stories about him.

THE TOMB OF NICHOLAS

According to this story, after Nicholas died and was buried in a marble tomb, instead of his body decaying, a fountain of oil streamed out from his head and a spring of water flowed from his feet. This holy water (very much like myrrh) was poured into bottles and made available to those who were afflicted by diseases. Many were healed as a result.

Some time later the man who had followed Nicholas as bishop became embroiled in church politics. Tempers flared, and the poor bishop was unable to satisfy either side. In the end, the warring parties ungraciously threw him out. That very day the holy water ceased to flow. As day followed day and those who were ill were turned away without the myrrh they came for, more and more of them began to say, "St. Nicholas is angry at us because we threw out his successor for no good reason!" And they turned on those who had expelled their bishop. It didn't take long for their message to get through. The good bishop was recalled to his post, and immediately the holy water began flowing again.

Why St. Nicholas's body did not decay is indeed a mystery, though he certainly is not unique in that respect. Throughout history, this phenomenon has occurred now and then. Such a saint is called a *myroblyte*. As for why it occurred with St.

Nicholas, Christina Hole theorizes that it was because of his great holiness that his body remained uncorrupted and gave forth the sweet-smelling essence known as "the manna of St. Nicholas," also known as "balm," "balsam," and "unguent."[2]

THE TWO GOLDEN GOBLETS

A number of stories, such as the following, have to do with attempts to outwit St. Nicholas:

A nobleman prayed, asking St. Nicholas for a son, promising the saint a golden goblet if his prayer were answered. A son was born to him, and the nobleman had a golden goblet made—but he liked it so much he had another made of equal value for the saint. During the voyage to Myra, the son fell overboard and disappeared while trying to fill the first goblet made with water. In sorrow, the father continued to Myra and laid down the second goblet at the altar. It fell from the altar as though repulsed. The second time the goblet was thrown even farther away. Then all present stared in amazement as the child arrived safe and sound, carrying the first goblet. He told them of St. Nicholas's care and protection. The joyful father then offered *both* goblets, and they were accepted.

NICHOLAS AND THE ARABIAN CONNECTION

After the Muslim invasion of the Mediterranean, life was never the same, especially for those who dwelt in coastal areas. For more than a thousand years, warfare between Muslims and Christians was almost continuous. The stories reflect that.

A number of the stories have to do with the Lycian coast during the years 824–954, when the Arabs controlled Crete. For 130 years, the nearby Asia Minor cities were never safe from attacks from that quarter. Of this period Jones wrote that

> each spring Crete vomited out like a monstrous war machine fleets of armored ships with black sails of marvelous speed. Cruising their *mare nostrum*, the freebooters burned cities and decimated towns before imperial forces could arrive. "Only hours sufficed for these remarkable corsairs, of agility, audacity, incomparable precision, to transform a flourishing Byzantine city into smoking ruins." The goods and slaves were marketed in the bazaars of the Asian and African coasts.[3]

Quite naturally, parents in Lycian cities felt utterly helpless to defend their families during this horrendous period. Since St. Nicholas came to be viewed as the premier defender against the Arabs, but whenever trouble from that quarter arrived, his was the first name to be invoked.

PRIEST FROM MYTILENE

It was St. Nicholas's feast day in Myra. A certain priest felt convicted to make a pilgrimage there. As he neared the city, he mingled with the crowd of pilgrims. After reaching the shrine of St. Nicholas, the priest heard some commotion outside. Suddenly, a man ran in, shouting, "Run for your lives!

Cretan Arabs have landed—and they're heading this way!" Immediately, everyone in the sanctuary made a rush for the door. Graciously, the priest let the others go first. By the time he reached the doorway, it was too late.

The Cretans were looking for slaves, women, children, and booty. All others they considered useless, and hence better off dead. First in line to be dispatched by the executioner was the priest. St. Nicholas was there, invisible to all except for the priest. Just as the sword was descending, the invisible hand of St. Nicholas wrenched the sword out of the executioner's hand and set the priest free.

BASILEOS

The following text was unearthed by author Martin Ebon:

Some years after the death of Saint Nicholas, the townspeople of Myra were celebrating his memory on the eve of his name-day, December 6, with eating, drinking, and a generally festive air. Unarmed and unaware of events around them, the towns-people did not realize that a band of Arab pirates from Crete had landed on their shore and was making its way into Myra. The pirates even managed to get into the Church of Saint Nicholas itself to collect booty in the form of chalices, altar decorations, and bejeweled icons. As they left town, they took along the son of a local peasant, Basileos, as a slave.

When the pirates returned to their home island, the emir of Crete selected young Basileos as his personal cupbearer.

But, back in Myra, his brokenhearted parents were inconsolable. It was terribly hard for them, a year later, to again celebrate December 6, but they eventually did so quietly at home.

Suddenly, the dogs began to bark fiercely. The father ever so cautiously opened the front door, and there was a ghostlike figure standing there: Basileos, dressed in an Arab tunic, holding a full goblet of wine in his hand, staring unseeingly into space.

Finally, Basileos, realizing he was home at last, told everyone how, while he was carrying a cup of wine to the emir, he had felt himself picked up by an invisible force. St. Nicholas had appeared in midair to give him courage, then accompanied him to Myra. The entire city rejoiced![4]

This story became a popular miracle play in the twelfth and thirteenth centuries and was adopted in a variety of settings. Interestingly enough, St. Nicholas did not exclude the Arabs from his services, as a number of stories evidence.

THE LONE SAILOR

This story has to do with an Egyptian Arab who ventured far out to sea one day in his fishing boat. Suddenly, a terrible storm blew in, and the little boat was tossed here and there as though it were but a chip of wood. Terrified, the fisherman invoked his gods, telling them that if they didn't quickly quell the storm, his boat would certainly sink. But these prayers were to no avail: the storm just got worse. Finally, as the boat was beginning to founder, the fisherman gave up on his gods and turned to St. Nicholas, figuring he had little to lose by changing allegiance. In his desperate prayer, he promised that if the saint would come to his rescue, he would become a Christian. The boat sank, but not before a figure swooped down and lifted him out of the boat, then bore him off to Attalia. Once on shore, his rescuer vanished, but later on the fisherman confirmed the identity of his rescuer by matching him to the picture on a St. Nicholas icon.

THE SARACEN TRADER

A Saracen trader was returning from a grueling but successful expedition to the Orient. How good it felt to finally be nearing home after such a long time on the trail! And the goods he was returning with would make him a rich man at the marketplace.

Then a wind came up. He wasn't apprehensive until it began to increase in intensity. Now he really began to worry, for he was traversing a dangerous mountain pass, where one misstep on the slippery rocks could be fatal. As the storm closed in, he could no longer even see the caravan behind him. His worst fears were realized when the camels behind him panicked and plunged off the trail into a deep abyss. The trader, having heard that St. Nicholas would come to the rescue of those who called upon him, concluded that he'd never need such assistance more than he did now, so he prayed to him.

Some time later, after the storm had abated, the ruined trader sorrowfully continued down the trail. Twelve miles farther on, as he came around a bend, what a sight met his eyes: his entire caravan (riders, camels, and goods) was there waiting for him!

When he reached his home in Seleucia, in gratitude the trader purchased an expensive golden icon of St. Nicholas and presented it to his city as a token of his deep appreciation.

≈

Contributing no little to the ecumenical persona of St. Nicholas was his willingness to respond to Arabs as well as Christians when they called upon him for help or mediation. However, this was in harmony with the post-apostolic teachings of reaching out to all peoples and all faiths.

6

SAINT NICHOLAS
MOVES WEST

Seven hundred years after the good saint died, he was still beloved throughout the East. His life story had been translated into Greek, Latin, Armenian, Syrian, Slav, and even Arabic. The Church of St. Nicholas was known and revered everywhere, and his December 6 feast day was widely observed, but the Byzantine Empire, subjected to continuous attacks from all directions, continued to shrink. Without that Byzantine bulwark, he'd soon be all but forgotten.

Enter the Normans. Fresh in their collective memory was a staggering event in the West, one of the most audacious attacks in history: France's invasion of England in 1066. Duke William of Normandy's fleet was broken up by a violent storm, and the entire coast of Normandy was strewn with the bodies of the drowned. The superstitious mariners urged him to call it quits, but the duke decided to invoke that interceding power sailors considered their last resort when disaster threatened: St. Nicholas. That very night, the wind changed, the waters calmed, and the remnants of the fleet sailed again. The showdown with England's King Harold, the Battle of Hastings, was considered by English historian Sir Edward Creasy to be one of the fifteen most pivotal battles in world history.[1] After his great victory, the duke (now surnamed "William the Conqueror"), remembering his promise to St. Nicholas, constructed "Battle Abbey" in gratitude to the bishop.[2]

That improbable turn of events was now followed by one just as significant—at least in terms of Christmas history. Bari, recently conquered by the Norman duke Robert Guiscard, felt seriously demoted because it was no longer the seat of Byzantine governors. About twenty years after William the Conqueror's invasion, a memorable "chamber of commerce" discussion apparently took place. These civic leaders yearned for their city to own a saint, which would mean instant status in the Christian community and, more to the point, would provide an ever-renewable resource: pilgrim tourists would visit, and visit, and visit again. But alas! Bari didn't own a saint—certainly not a bankable one. What to do to rectify such a sad situation?

So they began speculating on the already time-honored practice of stealing the bones of saints. Only *stealing* was too harsh a word; *abducted* was better, but the word *translation* sounded much more spiritually acceptable for such an act. It would take much too long to *grow* a saint, and they needed a saint . . . well, *now*.

Which reminded them of that heist of all heists: Venice's stealing of the bones of St. Mark from the city of Alexandria several centuries before. According to reports, certain civic-minded Venetians had held a meeting much like this one in Bari, in which they did mental searches of the locales where all the number one saints were buried or entombed. Along the way, St. Mark's name came up. He'd been entombed in Alexandria ever since his death in AD 68. But the Arabs had chased the Byzantines out of Egypt, and one of the Venetians just happened to remember that the new caliph of Egypt had recently demolished St. Mark's church in order to construct an opulent palace for himself on the site. Not being a "believer," most likely he didn't have the foggiest idea as to who St. Mark was.

That was all the listening Venetians needed to know—they immediately swung into action. The upshot was that, sometime in 828, a Venetian ship just happened to call on Alexandria. On board, under the command of the captain, was a crew armed with a map showing exactly where St. Mark's tomb could be found. They left nothing to chance: the guardian of the tomb was bribed—and bribed well.

The day of the abduction—*translation*—finally arrived. They'd thought of everything: a substitute body to dress up in whatever was covering St. Mark, a large wicker basket, pork (unclean in Islam), and cabbages to cover St. Mark's bones. Everything went off perfectly—except for the fragrance released from the opened crypt—but when concerned Alexandrians found St. Mark apparently still there, the

Venetians got away. And the rest was history: several hundred years of pilgrims by the thousands.

But now, rumor had it that Venice was looking for more saint-insurance in case of a drought of pilgrims, perhaps because of St. Mark's inexcusable failure to watch over his church. Ever since it burned down in 976, Venetians had been insecure, for his relics had never been found. Speculation had it that the Venetians were going after St. Nicholas next. And that's all the good citizens of Bari needed to galvanize them into action.

In the spring of 1087, a ship manned by seventy Barians landed at Myra, and they noted with joy that they'd beaten the Venetians. Dividing their group in two, twenty-three stayed on board to guard the ship, and the other forty-seven proceeded to the tomb. According to Nicephorus (a Benedictine monk), this is what happened. A similar account was chronicled by John, archdeacon of the Bari Cathedral. Both stories read like a Keystone Cops script.

Once at the tomb, they asked the monks who protected it where the body of St. Nicholas lay. Assuming they were there to show reverence to the saint, they gladly showed them where the body was. But then the monks, noting the size of the growing crowd, grew apprehensive, then angry. They now questioned the visitors sharply as to their intentions, saying, "You haven't planned to carry off the remnants of the holy saint to your own region, have you? If you have, we'll fight to the death to keep that from happening."

The Barians told the monks a whopping lie: that the pope

and all his archbishops and bishops had demanded that they journey to Myra and bring the body of St. Nicholas back to Bari. In fact, the saint had appeared in a dream to the pope himself, urging him to rescue his bones in all haste.

Seeing that the monks didn't believe a word of it, the Barians resorted to using force, shouldering the monks aside and forcing their way into the tomb. At this, some of the monks began to weep, and several others tried to sneak away to get help. The Barians put a quick stop to that by placing a guard around them.

One of the raiders, Matthew by name, now raised a huge mallet and hammered with great force on the tomb cover on the floor until he had shattered it. Underneath, a second cover was discovered. Matthew then beat on it until he had shattered it as well.

"And immediately such an odor was wafted up . . . that they seemed to be standing in Paradise."

At that, Matthew descended into the sacred tomb. Beholding the sacred remains "glowing like coals of fire, fragrant above all fragrance," he picked them up and kissed them endlessly before handing them up to Grimaldus and Lupus, the two Barian priests.

Meanwhile, the watching monks broke down in despair, but it was in vain. The armed abductors quickly hustled the relics down to their ship.

By this time, the inhabitants of the city were hurrying down to the harbor. Here they pled with the Barians to have mercy on them, they who had so faithfully watched over the saint for more than seven hundred years! And they waded into the water and tried to grasp any part of the ship they could hold on to. Alas! It was to no avail. The Barians placed the holy remains in a small wooden chest and sailed out of the harbor.

A storm, which some attributed to the work of St. Nicholas, forced the ship to pull into the harbor of Majesta. It was there that they realized some members of the expedition had already proven faithless and were hoarding portions of the relics. The captain refused to set sail until the ship had been searched top to bottom and the relics recovered.

Finally, after a long voyage, they arrived home. Runners were sent ahead into the city with the good news. By the time the ship drew into the harbor of Bari, on May 9, 1087, practically the entire city was at the dock, waiting for them.

Almost immediately there was trouble. Who would have custody of the precious relics? Some wanted to take them to the cathedral at once, and word was rushed to Archbishop Ursus. But Ursus was visiting in another town, so the mariners turned the relics over to Elias, the abbot of the Monastery of St. Benedict. But they didn't trust the abbot either, so they posted guards at the gates lest someone spirit the relics away from *them*.

When Ursus rushed back to Bari to claim the relics, the sailors and townspeople met him, teeth bared. The archbishop, unwilling to give in, decided to return later and take possession by force. In subsequent fighting, four died (two men from each side).

A large crowd of citizens now rescued the relics from the monastery, singing *Kyrie Eleison* all the while, and they brought them to the royal praetorium and placed them in the altar of St. Eustratius (the great martyr). And a large guard was posted to make sure the relics stayed *there*.

Then there came sick and lame people from all over the city; within twenty-four hours, forty-seven had been cured . . . and they kept coming.[3]

~

Historian Charles Jones maintains that there was ample reason to rush to completion this account—probably written within a week after May 9, 1087—by the Benedictine monk Nicephorus. "The party that at that moment possessed the relics, that is the Byzantine burghers, the crews that performed the feat, and the Greek aristocracy, were rushing into circulation that which would confirm their claim and their plans."[4]

Then we have the opposite party that was headed by Guiscard's chosen prelate, Archbishop Ursus. Had Ursus only known, he would have been there to meet the boat and awe the sailors into surrendering their precious burden. Instead, he was off on one of his many jaunts, and would spend the rest of his life regretting it. Here he was, building church after church, in order to shore up his reputation as an up-and-comer. Of this, Jones chortles, "It is one of the piquancies of true history, unmatched in legend, that the ambitious Ursus was caught absent from his post of duty at the most important moment of his life."[5] Interestingly enough, it took only two years for Ursus to lose his archbishopric to Abbot Elias!

Both sides were careful not to use the word *abduction* to define the act; rather, the word *translation* implied a higher power than the merchants/mariners was involved. But once translated, there was definitely very little peace in Bari. Possession being nine-tenths of the law, the citizens now had no intention of losing the fruits of all their labors. And the archbishop, his future prestige dependent on how he handled all this, and where the relics ended up, was openly angry about being squeezed out of the action. In the end, the deadlock had to be solved by a neutral, the Benedictine abbot Elias. Had there been a strong pope in power, and had Ursus been on the job when the ship landed, chances are that the St. Nicholas relics would have been housed in the Cathedral, but since that was not so, the basilica and tomb would be erected separately, all sides contributing.

On May 9, 1089, Pope Urban II consecrated the altar in the basilica that would take more than one hundred years to build. Thereafter May 9 would be celebrated as St. Nicholas Translation Day across the Mediterranean. At this dedication, it is likely that the first public appeal to Christian men to rally in defense of holy places in Palestine was made. It was Urban, by the way, who first promoted St. Nicholas as the church's only ecumenical figure with the power to unite East and West.

On Pentecost Sunday of 1137, Pope Innocent II presided over a magnificent service at the basilica in the presence of Emperor Lothar II and many German princes. And finally, more than a century since the altar had been consecrated, Chancellor Conrad of Hildesheim consecrated the completed facility on June 22, 1197. Also attending were five archbishops, twenty-eight bishops, and many clergy.

Many crusaders came to the tomb before leaving for the Holy Land. And before leaving for the East in 1096, almost all the great knights of the First Crusade traveled there to receive the blessing of St. Nicholas.[6]

The basilica is one of the most imposing and majestic churches in southern Italy, as well as one of the finest examples of Romanesque architecture in the world. According to art historians, it became the prototype of Apulian Romanesque for a great number of churches and cathedrals, through the centuries becoming one of the most important pilgrimage sites in the world.

SAINT NICHOLAS AT
FLOODTIDE

Everything, it seemed, was going right for the good bishop. And undoubtedly, the catalyst was the Bari relic translation, for not until that event took place did the cult of St. Nicholas really explode in the West. From that time on, St. Nicholas rode the crest, by 1400 becoming the most popular nonbiblical saint in Christendom. In fact, St. Nicholas is often depicted walking hand in hand with the Virgin Mary.

Sometime during the eleventh and twelfth centuries, all the legends of St. Nicholas having to do with his giving nature began to register in people's minds and bear fruit, especially his tendency to give in secret without thought of recognition or reward. So throughout Europe, people began giving gifts in the name of St. Nicholas. Nuns in France began the practice of surreptitiously leaving gifts for children at houses in the poorer parts of town on St. Nicholas Eve or St. Nicholas Day. Some were left in packages, others in stockings. Often included were good things to eat, such as fruits and nuts, or even oranges from Spain (a great luxury in those days).

The custom then spread like wildfire across Europe, gifts given now by rich and poor alike. In Oxford, by 1214, it was already a St. Nicholas Day custom to give bread, fish, and drink to the poorest children of the city. Some believed that St. Nicholas flew through the skies, looking for people who needed his help. When surprise gifts were given at celebrations and festivals, people began saying that they were gifts left by St. Nicholas.

St. Nicholas rode the lead wave into the Renaissance. He had already achieved preeminence in the East, but now, no small thanks to Bari, he achieved equal stature in the West. During these centuries, the shrine at Bari became almost as popular a pilgrim destination as Rome and St. James of Compostela. Especially attractive to pilgrims was the opportunity to acquire bottles of the sacred manna (or myrrh) emanating from the tomb. Then a rival St. Nicholas shrine established in Lorraine, France, St. Nicholas Port, swelled Nicholas-related pilgrimages even more.

Perhaps the best way of measuring the universality of St. Nicholas's position in history is to point out the groups who chose him as their patron saint. For starters, there were Constantinople and the Byzantine Empire, Moscow and the Russian Empire, Holland, Norway, eastern Italy, Lorraine, and New Amsterdam (Manhattan, New York). Dr. Adriaan De Groot notes that he was not only the protector of helpless infants and children but also the patron saint of parenthood, of barren wives who sought to have children, and of yearning virgins or spinsters who sought husbands.[1] He was the patron saint of bankers, moneylenders, and pawnbrokers; of students, scholars, pilgrims, and travelers; of butchers, mercers, and coopers; of thieves, murderers, pirates, prisoners, and vandals; of sailors, merchants, and fishermen; of sawyers, dyers, turners, haberdashers, and cartmakers; of seedmen, packers, chandlers, winers, drapers, and brewers; of ironmongers, coalmen, perfumers, and cobblers; of chemists, firemen, and crusaders; of clerks, clerics, orphans, and royalty. He was always the protector of the weak against the strong, the poor against the rich, and, not coincidentally, the patron saint of giving and Christmas.

~

Several of the stories have to do with the impact St. Nicholas had on crusaders during the eight Crusades that turned the Mediterranean world upside down during the eleventh, twelfth, and thirteenth centuries. In the end, the Christians lost Jerusalem again, they all but destroyed their Christian allies in Constantinople, the previously tolerant Arabs were now intolerant of all dissent, and the church bore the brunt of what was widely perceived as a fiasco. "Mohammed," jested the skeptics, "has proven stronger than Christ."

Nevertheless, since most of the crusaders journeyed through Bari en route to the Holy Land, and few proceeded on without praying at the basilica of St. Nicholas, the crusaders did not discredit Nicholas. Indeed the cult of St. Nicholas exploded across Europe as a direct result.

IMPRISONED IN GAZA

One crusader, Cunon de Richecourt, was taken prisoner in Gaza (1240). He prayed continually to St. Nicholas, urging him to help release him. On St. Nicholas Eve, 1244, his prison door suddenly opened; next thing he knew, he was standing in his chains in front of the door of the Church of Saint Nicolas de Port in Lorraine, France. In gratitude for his deliverance, the Lord of Richecourt funded a torchlight procession to take place every December 5 between 8:00 a.m. and 9:00 p.m., promising to be present for it every St. Nicholas Eve for the rest of his life.

BLACK FALCON

This is one Crusader story that almost ran away with Charles Jones. Initially, he just couldn't believe it; it seemed too far-fetched to be true. But the more he researched it, the more convinced he became that it was historically accurate. It features two larger-than-life superheroes: Fulk Nerra (the "Black Falcon") and his son, Geoffrey Martel ("the Hammer"), founders of the House of Anjou that filled so many thrones of Europe.

Fulk Nerra was described by A. LeMoy as "a strange and complex figure, indefatigable, athirst for vengeance, brutal in moments of reprisal, quick to remorse, hurrying to Palestine [as penance for crimes committed], making his own servants beat him, and despite those penances always the bandit, builder of castles and churches, including some marvels, feared and adored by all, uniting in his person all contracts."[2]

Fulk, also called Anjou, started out with a piece of land about fifty miles square. He had no pushover neighbors: to his north was Normandy and Maine; to his east, Chartres and Blois; to the south, Poitou; and to the west, the kingdom of Brittany. But in fifty-three years of rule, friend and foe alike trembled at his coming. By the time his son Geoffrey died, Anjou held the balance of power in all of France. It was even said that William the Conqueror attacked England rather than face the Anjous. When Fulk's first wife, Elizabeth of Vendôme, failed to produce a son, he had her put to death. Same treatment to Hugh of Beauvais, the favorite of King Robert Capet: Fulk and his knights slew him right in front of the king himself. After acts such as these, Fulk became terrified that he was headed straight for hell, and so he would go on journeys to Palestine for more penance.

On one of these trips, off the Antiochene coast, the ship Fulk was in was engulfed by a terrific storm. Each man aboard, anticipating death, invoked his favorite saint. Since Fulk heard the name of Nicholas being invoked all around him, he fell on his knees, promising St. Nicholas that if he'd only spare his life, he'd build a church in honor of him when he returned to France. The storm died down, and not long after, Fulk made his way home, stopping on the way to visit the pope. After returning to France, he built a monastery in honor of St. Nicholas, and it was this monastery that began the cult of St. Nicholas in western France.

In his later years, Fulk's son by his second wife, Adela Geoffrey, revolted against him. The old man not only defeated his son; he forced him to carry a saddle on his back for a number of days, finally collapsing on it in exhaustion. Fulk rose up and kicked his prostrate son, exclaiming, *"Victus es tandem, victus!"* ["You're still beaten! Beaten!"]. The son calmed his father down by saying that no one else on earth could vanquish him but his father.

Once again Fulk journeyed to far-off Jerusalem, where he commanded two servants to drag him naked, in the sight of the Turks, to the Holy Sepulcher, scourging him all the way, while he cried out, "Lord, receive the wretched Fulk, Thy perfidious scoundrel; look to my repentant soul, O Lord Jesus Christ." The mercurial count died returning from this last trip to Jerusalem. However, the St. Nicholas Abbey remained, and it was a powerful cultural force for centuries.[3]

≈

Other St. Nicholas stories reflect Europe's growing secularization, greatly accelerated by both the Crusades and the Renaissance.

DAZED THIEVES

During a local war, the wife of a prefect hid two sacks of valuable goods in the balcony of the local St. Nicholas church. Two boys hunting for birds' nests in the church found the sacks. They determined to return that night when no one would be around to see them. That night they hauled off the two sacks but got lost in the woods. When they finally *did* find their way out, lo and behold, directly ahead of them, there was the church. Again they tried to find their way home; again they got lost and ended up at the church. At dawn, having once again returned to the church, they resignedly dropped the sacks in the churchyard and ran, this time finding their homes. A neighbor caught them trying to wash away the grime accumulated during the night and made them confess. The prefect and his wife recovered their property and fervently thanked St. Nicholas for his protection.

THE MONK OF EYNSHAM

It is said that Adam, abbot of the Abbey of Eynsham from AD 1213 to 1228, was the author of a highly valued account of the vision of Edmund the monk of Eynsham. Adam wrote that on the Thursday before Easter in 1196, a young monk named Edmund fell into a forty-hour trance and only returned to life on Saturday evening. The vision he had during his trance went on to become one of the most famous and influential medieval works of the genre. In fact, many believe it was a model for Dante. Like Dante's, Edmund's vision takes place at Eastertide and involves a contest for souls. Jones describes the action in these words:

Though pilgrim and guide first travel through a schematized Hell, the center of interest is Purgatory, a hill as in Dante. In the journey through it the redeemed have their burdens lightened. The therapy is homeopathic. Specific clerics and even a pope are punished. The transition from misery to health is gradual, and during it the greatest suffering results from uncertainty of salvation. Periods of purgation are fixed periods of time, though the periods are shorter than Dante's. There are the same nightly rests.

The guide, equivalent with Virgil, is N [Nicholas], who leads Edmund not only through Hell and Purgatory but Paradise as well. . . . According to Matthew Paris, ten years after the Eynshan vision, Thurcill of Essex had a vision in which Saint Julian was guide; in that instance N was an overseer of Purgatory, not wholly unlike the Cato figure of Dante.[4]

THE BARI WIDOW

Might Chaucer also have been influenced by the St. Nicholas stories? This tale is thought by some to have inspired Chaucer's *Troilus and Criseyde*, possibly even "The Miller's Tale" and "The Prioress's Tale" of his *Canterbury Tales*. Jones feels it was composed somewhere around 1150.

It begins with "There was a man of noble birth and handsome features," who lived in Bari not too long after the St. Nicholas translation. This clerk ran a school in that city. "In that same city lived a widow preeminently endowed in mind, though even richer in wealth and loveliness. In either grace she was so surpassing that by a look she could have enticed a stony Demosthenes to the nuptial bed or aroused passion in the most chaste Lucrece." But this widow was both chaste and true, and she venerated all the saints—but St. Nicholas most of all. In fact, she frequently held vigils next to the saint's tomb.

Well, it took but one look for the clerk (cleric) to be "stricken to the marrow." He was in anguish and torment from continually desiring her. And the more he tried to smother the flame, the more it grew. Soon his face had become distorted by his continual lustful thoughts. Finally, he gave up and confessed his love to the beautiful widow, only to be rejected.

At a dinner party the widow held annually on St. Nicholas Day, she berated the clerks for their failure to compose "a single responsory or prose suitable for praise of that good friend of God, or even a canticle to joyfully honor his festive holy day." The languishing clerk heard about her challenge and quickly composed a composition honoring St. Nicholas, for he had reasons for wanting to win. Unwisely, the widow had promised "any gift" to the clerk who could create an acceptable St. Nicholas *historia*.

The clerk then wrote a splendid *historia*, which awed all who studied it, including the delighted widow, who asked him to name his reward. He demanded her love. Nothing could dissuade him in his determination to have her at all costs—not money, not power, not anything. He gave her but one day before delivering herself to him.

The brokenhearted and shamed widow wept most of that

twenty-four hours; all that night she prayed that Nicholas would somehow save her from the clerk's demands. Meanwhile, the young clerk lay awake cursing the time he had to wait before the widow became his mistress. Suddenly, St. Nicholas entered his room, seized him by the hair, and began lashing him with his whip. Though the saint's face radiated compassion, there was no compassion in his whip. Nor in his words of condemnation. Finally, the thoroughly cowed young man exclaimed, "Lord, have mercy on me a sinner." At this, St. Nicholas identified himself and told him that the floggings would not stop until he promised to release the widow from her promise and to cease demanding that she give in to his lustful desires. Quickly, the chastened young man got up, went to St. Nicholas's tomb, found the weeping widow, and begged for her forgiveness. The widow granted that forgiveness, and both lived out their lives in devotion to the saint, the widow founding a convent.[5]

THE CROSS LEGEND

This is the second St. Nicholas story to refer to the Reginold Eichstätt *historia* that was then sweeping across Europe. The original account was penned by John the Deacon.

In the story, the Nicholas *historia* was being sung, whistled, and performed everywhere, but not in the Saint Mary of Charity cloister. Their prior, Dom Ytherius, was finally approached by the senior monks and asked if he would permit them to "psalm the responses of the blessed Nicholas." The prior not only rejected their request; he did it angrily. Surprisingly, the monks pressed him on the issue, with words such as these: "Why, father, do you disdain to listen to your sons? Why, when the *historia* of Saint Nicholas, full of sweet spiritual honey, is already honored through nearly the whole globe, cannot we chant it? Why cannot we, like others, be refreshed at such a feast? . . . Why, with all the churches committed to jubilation through this new leaven, must this cell alone now remain in mute silence?"

Finally, the prior exploded with blasphemies and ordered them out.

But that night, St. Nicholas appeared to the prior and castigated him in no uncertain terms. Not contenting himself with that, the good saint dragged him off his cot by his hair and shoved him down on the dormitory floor. Then he began singing the Nicholas anthem, *O pastor aeterne*, and with each modulation he lashed the neck of the unfortunate prior with a whip that the saint had thoughtfully remembered to bring along. Eventually, the thoroughly beaten prior got the message and learned the words to St. Nicholas's satisfaction. By now nearly hysterical from all he had gone through, the prior began to sob loudly. Hearing this, the brothers ran into the room and were amazed to find the prior prone on the floor. He was unable to provide them with a satisfactory explanation as to what was wrong with him, so they carried him into the infirmary, where he remained for some days.

At last, restored to health by the intervention of the good saint, he summoned all the brothers and announced some unexpected news: "Observe, my dearest sons, that after I refused to obey you I underwent severe punishment for my hardness of heart. Now do I not only freely accord with your request, but as long as I live I will be the first and most accomplished chanter of the *historia* of that great father."[6]

THE THREE CHILDREN IN THE SALT TUB

This particular story is one of the most famous, and oft-painted, stories about St. Nicholas. It also has many variations, both in subject matter and in geographical area. Several centuries later, the protagonists are three small children instead of the students in this earlier version.

Three theology students were traveling through France. As they saw night approaching, they started looking for a place to spend the night. Finally they reached an inn, and gratefully entered it and asked for a room. The sharp-eyed innkeeper observed that their purses were heavy. Late that night, after they were all asleep, he softly entered their room. So soundly were they sleeping that they didn't notice when he stole their purses. Not content with theft, however, the innkeeper killed them, perhaps by smothering them with a pillow. Then he surreptitiously carried each one downstairs to the meat room. There he stripped them, cut them up into slices, and put those slices into casks used for salting meat. Variant accounts portray the innkeeper's wife as an accomplice.

The next morning St. Nicholas arrived. Some versions have him ordering breakfast and catching the innkeeper and his wife in the act of preparing the slices of students for cooking. In others, he demands that the innkeeper take him to the room where the dismembered students are. Then St. Nicholas accused him of murder. When the innkeeper denied it, St. Nicholas restored the students to life in front of his very eyes.

THE BURTSCHEID ICON

Not long before the year 1000, Emperor Otto III built a monastery at Burtscheid not far from Charlemagne's capital of Aachen. Otto appointed a monk named Gregory as abbot. Gregory built two chapels, one dedicated to St. Apollinaris, the other to St. Nicholas. The abbot also acquired a St. Nicholas icon that had been painted in Constantinople. Supposedly it was carried west by the son of the king of Greece.

On one occasion, it was carried to the house of a noblewoman who was about to be delivered of a child, and hung on the wall opposite her bed. During her delivery, in the sight of all who were present, the picture turned its face to the wall, as though to avoid seeing the woman in her labor.

This story is the earliest evidence we have of St. Nicholas's connection with childbirth.

HOW THE GOOD GIFTS WERE USED BY TWO

Few people are aware that famed nineteenth-century artist Howard Pyle was also extremely interested in preserving (and illustrating) folk tales from around the world. This story is very much in the Grimm Brothers tradition. It is a fascinating rarity in St. Nicholas stories: it gives equal billing to another saint— St. Christopher:

Once upon a time there was a rich brother and a poor brother, and the one lived across the street from the other. The rich brother had all of the world's gear that was good for him, and more besides; the poor brother had hardly enough to keep soul and body together, yet he was contented with his lot. One day who should come traveling to the town where the rich brother and the poor brother lived but St. Nicholas himself.

As chance would have it, St. Nicholas knocked at the rich brother's house first. St. Nicholas had walked a long way that day so was dusty and rather disreputable-looking. The rich brother gaped like a toad in a rain-storm and directed him to seek lodging across the street.

This St. Nicholas did, and was right royally welcomed in. The good wife spread before him all that they had in the house: a loaf of brown bread and a crock of cold water from the town fountain. So the saint asked them to bring him an empty bowl and crock. Then he blessed them and said, "Bowl, be filled!" and immediately the bowl began to boil up with a good rich meat pottage. When it was full to the brim, he said, "Bowl, be stilled," and it stopped making broth. Then he turned to the crock and said, "Crock, be filled!" and it bubbled up with the purest of crystal water, only stopping with the command, "Crock, be stilled!" Then everyone ate and drank till there was no room for more. The next morning, St. Nicholas left them, but there was now no danger of hunger or thirst ever returning to that house.

One day, the rich brother got his brother to tell him the whole story while he watched the bowl and crock at work. He decided that he *had* to have them for himself! After repeated "No's" from his brother, he finally purchased them for a large sum of money.

The next day, the rich brother told his wife *he* would take care of dinner that day rather than she. At dinner-time, he gave the command, and sure enough, the bowl and crock were soon filled. Unfortunately, he didn't remember how to stop the process, so soon the broth and water filled the entire room, then the entire house—so the rich brother ran across the street and demanded to be told how to stop the process before the entire town was engulfed. But the poor brother was not to be rushed. Only after being paid another large sum of money would the poor brother agree to take back the bowl and crock.

Some time later, St. Christopher was thinking about taking a little journey to earth. St. Nicholas suggested that if he wanted real hospitality, he should drop by the poor brother's house. But when he arrived in town, the rich brother's house looked so much larger and finer that he knocked there first. The door was opened, then slammed in his face. So he went across the street and knocked there. He was warmly welcomed in, fed from the bowl and crock, and given a comfortable bed. The good wife had noticed how tattered St. Christopher's shirt was, so she spent much of the night making a new shirt for him. It was there by his bedside when he woke up.

Before he left, the poor brother emptied his stocking full of silver on the table, and told him to take all he needed of it. In gratitude, St. Christopher left him with a blessing, saying, "Whatever it be that you begin doing this morning, you shall continue doing until sunset." After he left, the wife decided to fold what new linen she had left after making the shirt, and her husband decided to put what was left of the silver away. So they did, but they couldn't quit: by the time evening came, the house was full of fine linen and every tub and bucket was brimming over with silver money!

When the rich brother came over, how his eyes bugged out with greed! He demanded that if either of the saints ever returned, he should be given first chance to offer them hospitality. Well, a year and a day passed, and both saints came to the poor man's door, who asked if they'd mind staying with the rich brother across the street. Rather grudgingly, they knocked on the other door. My! What a difference this time! They were given a great feast, new clothes were laid out for them, and next morning they were offered as much gold as they could stuff into their pockets. In return, they were left the same blessing as that left for the poor brother, and then their celestial visitors left.

The rich brother's wife decided that before she began to fold fine linen all day, she'd better feed the pigs and fill their water troughs. The rich man was so envious of his brother that he wanted to get even more silver than he had, but couldn't figure out how to do it. So he just sat there and smoked. Some time later he sought out his wife, and lo, there she was pouring out water for the pigs. That made him so furious he picked up a switch and struck his wife with it. And both of them continued doing so until evening. In the meantime, all the neighbors came out to see what the hubbub was all about and laughed until they cried. In the evening they had nothing to show for the visit of St. Nicholas and St. Christopher but a wet pig and a badly bruised back!

For "even the blessed saints cannot give wisdom to those who shut their eyes to it."[7]

Interestingly, there was another saint who was often paired with St. Nicholas, Catherine of Alexandria, a post-apostolic fourth-century martyr. Catherine and Nicholas together are the leading tutelary saints of scholars and schools.[8] They are also the most popular names given to girl/boy twins.

THE ACCIDENT OF BIRTH

This is the only story that features St. Nicholas's relationship with the storks. It begins with these words:

"Saint Nicholas used to send, so I am told,
    All new-born babes by storks, in days of old."

In the story, King Friedrich Max of Stultzenmannekim prayed for many years that St. Nicholas would send a baby boy to him and his queen. Finally, St. Nicholas called Wilhelm Stork (a very sober bird) and told him to deliver a baby boy to the queen. But Wilhelm Stork was old and hard of hearing, so ended up delivering the young prince to a cobbler who already had a half dozen children of his own![9]

~

One can't help but notice in these stories that St. Nicholas is portrayed as a rather mercurial saint, oscillating between kindness and cruelty, giving and taking, blessing and punishing. Church historian Ancelet-Hustache explains the paradox in this way:

On one hand the beneficent saint, the light-bringing apparition; on the other, the enemy of mankind, the dark dweller in dark places. Nothing could be more in tune with the spirit of the Middle Ages than this violent contrast. The art and literature of the period, the legends, "miracles" and other dramatic "games"—all included the devil. The people of medieval days loved depicting the devil as hideously as they could, as we can see from the sculptures in the cathedrals, stressing the horns and claws, so that his final defeat might be all the more glorious. They saw the saints as their powerful assistants in their unceasing struggle against the Evil One, and above all they expected help from St. Nicholas, whom they placed so high in the hierarchy of heaven. Emperor Leo the Wise, who was writing in the tenth and eleventh centuries, summed up the thought of his time and the centuries to come when he wrote that the Enemy suffered a defeat whenever any saint's feast was celebrated, but that the feast of St. Nicholas caused him the greatest trouble, for it was celebrated all over the world.[10]

Normally, St. Nicholas, being a chaste ascetic, has very little to do with the fair sex. And certainly there is not even a hint that he would intervene in a case where lust was a factor. "The Bari Widow" builds a case for his being a protector of woman's virtue, as does the much earlier story of "The Three Dowerless Daughters."

"The Three Children in the Salt Tub/Young Theology Students" story does a number of things: it strengthens the case for St. Nicholas's Trinitarian credentials, and it reinforces his position as a protector of children, students, and clerics, depending on who the protagonist in the story was. Since the story appeared late (in the twelfth century), and only in the West, the assumption is that it was intended to fill a felt need, a gap, in the St. Nicholas story canon. The story was also incorporated into several miracle plays, and artists all across Europe depicted the story in hundreds of paintings, sculptures, stained-glass windows, and bas-reliefs.

"The Burtscheid Icon" is especially intriguing, as it reflects the time's attitude toward partial nudity and childbirth. Even the St. Nicholas icon is so prudish that it turns itself over on the hook to avoid seeing the scene! In the companion childbirth story, "The Accident of Birth," St. Nicholas is clearly singled out as the patron saint of childbirth, regardless of station in life.

And "The Cross Legend" tells of an overprotective saint who is so invested in the success of music dedicated to him that he is willing to whip anyone who fails to sing his praises. In fact, the whipping aspect of these last two stories reveals St. Nicholas in a most unflattering light. But perhaps they do bridge to the later punishing dimension represented by assistants to St. Nicholas such as *Belsnickel*, *Perre Fouettard*, *Krampus*, and Black Pete.

With these stories, we bring St. Nicholas through the medieval and Renaissance periods. By and large, we note a diminution of miraculous elements. Furthermore, we are introduced to characters who sound so natural to us they could well be contemporaries of ours.

8

FIGHTING FOR SURVIVAL

The fall of the Byzantine Empire in 1453 proved to have unexpected consequences, for with it, the once unassailable marriage of political authority and religious authority sanctioned by Emperor Constantine collapsed too. Suddenly the church was forced to defend what it had for so long taken for granted. All the abuses in the system came to a head at once, including the undeniable fact that the church had become a great temporal power, claiming or controlling a minimum of one quarter of all the land in Europe. In effect it had become a state within each state. With all this, the Protestant Reformation ignited by Martin Luther was almost a foregone conclusion.

Before we go on, this would be the perfect place to address the issue of sainthood by retracing its biblical and subsequent history.

Sainthood has a much longer and richer history than is generally known. For starters, Old Testament writers used the term often to describe men and women of exceptional holiness, integrity, and consecration—also known for their compassion, goodness, and godliness. Interestingly enough, throughout Old Testament times *all* followers of God were labeled "saints." Saints are referred to sixty times in the New Testament. The difference appears to be that now saints are subdivided into two categories: those who are still living their mortal lives, and those who are supernaturally alive in heaven with God, and who will return with Jesus Christ at the Second Coming.

Using the same criteria favored by biblical writers, post-apostolic Christians labeled such men and women "saints." Canonization (to declare a deceased person an officially recognized saint) did not occur until later. *Britannica* editors point out that there was no such thing as formal canonization in the early Christian church. Over time, early Christians separated Christians who died natural deaths from those who were martyred for their faith—from the latter came those they elevated (personally and collectively) into the pantheon of "saints"; also considered a gilt-edged credential for sainthood was suffering greatly for one's faith, usually during times of persecution; Nicholas would gain entry to this most selective group of honorees through his incarceration during the great persecution instigated by Emperor Diocletian.

As for the Roman Catholic Church, papal canonization did not even begin until 993 when Pope John XV declared Ulric of Augsburg to be a saint. Over time, it became understood within the Catholic Church membership that only popes had the power to canonize. By the twelfth and thirteenth centuries, the procedures became so streamlined and predictable that sainthood for those perceived to be exceptionally godly came faster and faster after death (often within only a year or two). What this means is that post-apostolic Christians and early church martyrs became known as saints, not by a formal process of canonization, but by common consent among Christian believers.

Today, many scholars—even Catholic scholars—believe that formal canonization should have been left theoretical rather than making it a prerogative of reigning popes. For had that not been true, Protestants would not have had reason to discredit and throw out *all* saints during the Reformation (not just those canonized by popes but also all those so elevated during the first thousand years or so after Christ's Ascension who were now damned through guilt by association). Then there was Vatican II, when the entire process of canonization was placed under modern microscopes, resulting in many, such as St. Nicholas— who had been canonized later by the Catholic Church—being after-the-fact stripped of sainthood. All this has generated cynicism about the entire process, not to mention fury by all those who love and revere those figures now discredited.

Nicholas was already the exception, and not the rule, however.

WHY NICHOLAS IS DIFFERENT

Normally, saints are canonized only after at least being first beatified, which means to declare a person to have attained the blessedness of heaven, to authorize the title "blessed," and to authorize limited public religious honor. The three main criteria for beautification are as follows: (1) establish a reputation for sanctity; (2) establish the heroic quality of the virtues; (3) prove the working of miracles (validation by a committee of cardinals of at least two specific miracles).

Orthodox Christians also have a history of canonization. Protestants generally do not, feeling more comfortable with the broader use of the term time-honored by biblical writers.

What many fail to realize, however, is that one of the reasons Nicholas was being stripped of his "sainthood" by Vatican II is the key reason why he's stayed alive for seventeen hundred years: he became a "saint" not because he'd performed a string of miracles or died a martyr, but because his entire life-ministry was constructed on one simple principle. In every act of his life, his template of action was taken from Christ's own words—whatever it is that you do for others, do it anonymously. One cannot receive credit in two places at once. Get credit on earth, or get credit in heaven—you get only one choice. So with this as a preamble, let's see how the issue of sainthood affected the status and role of St. Nicholas.

As ideological differences were hammered into creeds, and Europe was subjected to centuries of bloody conflict in the name of those creeds, the proverbial baby tended to be thrown out with the bathwater; in this case, the saints—saints such as St. Nicholas. Apparently, it mattered little that the process of canonization had not really gained momentum until after AD

1000, or that saints such as Nicholas dated clear back to post-apostolic times. Most of the figures that had been revered for so long by the church were now discarded by Protestants who sought to eradicate all things associated with the Roman Catholic Church, and they fired their big guns at sainthood. Jones notes that "they attacked no instinct or perception so hardily as that of *mediation*: they asserted that the God-Man alone could mediate, not one of His creatures like the Church, and certainly not the saints. . . . Many, even within Catholicism, believed the Church would have done well to leave canonization or any other judgment of sanctity to the direct action of the holy Spirit."[1]

So what did it all mean to St. Nicholas, the erstwhile patron saint of *everybody*? Was his mission on earth complete? Paradoxically, it turned out that the very people responsible for heaving him out ended up being the ones who rather red-facedly brought him back.

And the catalyst was Christmas, till then merely one item in Nicholas's bulging portfolio. The issue of Christmas proved to be far more explosive than the Reformers had anticipated: if St. Nicholas was no longer the patron saint of Christmas, who was? Who indeed? Initially, Luther himself had continued to give presents to his children and household on St. Nicholas Day, but later ceased doing so. Then the Reformation leaders cast around for a suitable replacement. Finally, one of them came up with the brilliant idea that that role ought to be given to the Christ child Himself. So they enthusiastically made that change happen. But biblically, the Christ child was the *receiver* of gifts rather than being the *giver*. Even more frustrating to Protestant leaders was that their own families rebelled against them. Worse yet, they hadn't thought through cause and effect enough to realize that nature abhors a vacuum and that the cure in this case might end up being far worse than the disease.

What none of them apparently realized was that evicting St. Nicholas from the Christmas season, through the front door, would result in a host of jubilant pagan deities rushing in through the back door. Thus, the act of evicting St. Nicholas opened up the long-shut Pandora's box. Instead of making the observance of Christmas more sacred as they assumed it would, it resulted in secular pagan deities replacing the post-apostolic one. Ruefully, the Reformers discovered they'd grossly underestimated the saint's resilience and the hold he had on the minds, hearts, and souls of Christians everywhere—and St. Nicholas's protean ability to reshape his persona without completely losing the magic that had kept him alive for more than a thousand years. Luther himself had to end up admitting defeat by contritely announcing that henceforth St. Nicholas would be the messenger who relays to the Christ child all requests for presents. But that compromise didn't work either. The *Christkindel* persona never really worked, for people soon recognized how contrived the very concept was.

When the *Christkindel* failed to fill St. Nicholas's considerable shoes, just who were these pagan or semi-pagan deities that flooded in to fill the vacuum? First and foremost, every last one of them were mythical contrivances; none were real people.

One of them was *Befana*, a genial hag that predated Christianity. Christians in southern Europe now retrofitted her as a fourth (and nonbiblical) member of the Magi. Her Russian counterpart was known as *Baboushka*. Then there was *Berchta*, a hook-nosed German counterpart to *Befana; Knecht Ruprecht*, a German fertility relic of winter solstice celebrations; *Nissen*, a ghoulish Dane with a long, red tongue and big tail; the Austrian goatman *Krampus*; and kinsmen such as *Hans Trapp* (Alsace-Lorraine), Black Pete (Low Countries), *Pere Fouettard* (France), *Tompte Gubbe* (Sweden), *Hoêscker* (Luxembourg), *Bartel* (Silesia), and Germanic figures such as *Rue Klaus, Hans Muff, Gumphinkel, Pelznickel, Aschen Klaus*, and *Butterman*.

And also there were those who actually impersonated St. Nicholas, figures such as *Pere Noel* (French Father Christmas), *Weihnachtsmann* (German Christmas Man), and England's Father Christmas.

As for *Christkindel*, in Spain he was called *Niño Jesus*; in France, *Petit Noel*; in Italy, *Gesu Bambino*; and in America, he mutated through three feminine age-level stages (baby, small girl, teenage girl) into a male St. Nicholas: *Kris Kringle*.

HOLLAND: KEEPER OF THE
ST. NICHOLAS FLAME

As the world moved into the sixteenth, seventeenth, and eighteenth centuries, and the fallout from the Protestant Reformation continued to play out, what happened to St. Nicholas? Society continued to grow ever more secular, accelerated by scientific debunking of much of what had been accepted as truth. And functions once filled by church and family were more and more preempted by the state. In such a world, it would seem obvious that there would be precious little room for a personage such as St. Nicholas.

Enter Holland. Holland has never wavered in its commitment to St. Nicholas. None of the substitutes trotted out by Protestant reformers found much of a welcome among the Dutch people. Not only was St. Nicholas already a fixture by the 1300s, but he has remained so ever since.

One Dutch artist contributed more than all the rest to making permanent St. Nicholas's hold on Europe's lowland peoples—Jan Steen (1626–1679). Unquestionably, Steen's famous painting *The Eve of St. Nicholas* is the most significant of all Nicholas-related art.

As was true in other European countries, St. Nicholas's persona continued to evolve in Holland, Belgium, and other lowland countries. Only here, the most significant changes came not in the good saint himself but in his sidekick, Black Pete. As we have seen, Black Pete was originally not only repulsive but positively ghoulish—almost the devil incarnate. But over the centuries, the Dutch ever so gradually wore off his rough edges. So much so that it's difficult to tell today which is more popular in Holland, St. Nicholas or the irrepressible, cavorting Black Pete, who does his best to upset his master at every possible opportunity.

Black Pete's origins are indistinct: possibly Turkish, but more likely Moorish. Since Holland was occupied for an extended period of time by Spanish imperial forces, they impacted historical figures such as St. Nicholas. Over time, the tradition developed that Nicholas was not from Turkey at all, but from Spain. Indeed, he and Black Pete supposedly spend most of every year in Spain; then every mid-November they leave Spain by ship and land, with great fanfare, in Holland, where they then rule supreme over Nicholastide, not leaving until that season is over. On St. Nicholas Eve, the saint and Black Pete ride the Dutch skies, landing on housetop after housetop, listening in at chimneys, and leaving gifts. St. Nicholas always rides his great white horse. His magical robe gives him the power to travel in the twinkling of an eye wherever he and Black Pete wish to go. Nowhere in the world is Nicholastide celebrated with more excitement, warmth, and joie de vivre than in the Low Countries.

But the Dutch as a people must bear the responsibility and consequences for transplanting the good saint into the fertile soil of the New World, undoubtedly the most fascinating development ever in the Nicholas saga. Let's find out how it happened.

9

SAINT NICHOLAS IN THE NEW WORLD

St. Nicholas would cross the Atlantic as two personas: one as the *Belsnickel*, with German immigrants; the other as *Sinterklaas*, with Dutch/Walloon immigrants.

BELSNICKEL/CRISTKINDEL

In German communities in the New World, the *Belsnickel* and *Christkindel* operated as a team. The grotesque-looking, furry *Belsnickel* and the angelic, feminine *Christkindel* proved to be a most effective combination of violence and softness, and thus mirrored most of the commonly accepted attributes of the secularized Nicholas/Black Pete in Europe's Low Countries.

German migration to America really began when William Penn invited his continental neighbors to immigrate to his British colony in 1682—Penn's Woods, or Pennsylvania. By

1689, several thousand Germans had moved to the new colony; by 1742, one hundred thousand had arrived—and by 1783, almost three hundred thousand. Eventually, more than one-third of Americans would have German in their ancestry.

Both Roman Catholic and Lutheran Germans brought *Christkindel* and *Pelsnickel* with them. (Keep in mind that anything with "nickel" in it translates "Nicholas," a shortened version of the name.) Only in America, the *P* was dropped over time and the *B* was substituted, hence *Belsnickel*. The use of "nickel" enabled Germans to give a double meaning to the name, as the ancient meaning of the word encompassed "fur demon," "fur imp," and a devil-like aspect. In portions of Germany, he was called *Pelsmartel* (in honor of Martin Luther), and his visit was tied to Luther's birthday on November 11. *Pelsnickel*, on the other hand, would come on December 5, the Eve of St. Nicholas.

Later on Christmas Eve the *Christkindel* supposedly would return when all were asleep and enter the house through an open window, a keyhole, the fireplace (rarely), or through the walls, and would place the gifts on the table—*not* under a tree—in the Christmas room. Although it was known that she came on a donkey or a mule with great light around her, no one was privileged actually to see her during those later deliveries of presents and coins.

So angelic was the *Christkindel* that it is easy to see why her visits were perceived as spiritual ones. The time varied, but usually it would be Christmas Eve, after the lamps were lit, when one of the *Christkindel*'s companions would ring a bell in front of the window. Then after establishing contact with those inside, the question would be asked: "May the *Christkindel* come in?" Answered in the affirmative by the lady of the house, the entourage would enter, and almost immediately the *Christkindel* would begin questioning the children as to their behavior during the year.

Children would often be frightened by all this commotion. They would be asked standard questions such as "Have you obeyed your parents all this year?" "Have you said your prayers every night?" If they had been good, they were rewarded with gifts. If they had been bad, they'd receive blows or be switched. Some *Christkindels* would affect great doubt about the regularity of their prayer life, causing all the children to fall on their knees and recite their prayers as proof of their assertions, just as St. Nicholas would have done.

If there were children who had misbehaved—usually recalcitrant boys—a signal would be given that would summon the *Belsnickel*. In the early days the two traveled together. The *Belsnickel* would usually be a strong male with a deep, booming bass voice. He would be covered by a shaggy fur coat (often with the fur worn on the inside). Generally, he would either wear a grotesque mask or his face would be blackened with burnt cork.

On his back would be a long chain that rattled terribly when he wished to frighten, and in one hand was a bundle of switches. Oftentimes he'd wear patchwork clothes—everything he wore or carried was of antique vintage—and carry a large bow and a quiver of arrows. Attached to his long coattails would be bells. His stockings would be of green buckram, on his feet would be Indian moccasins, around his ample waist was a wide belt, and on his head would be an ancient hat worn low over his forehead. His old clothes would be ill-fitting, so pillows often would exaggerate the already well-nourished figure. If he was beardless, he would most likely don an artificial one; above it would be his trademark: a sinister, upward-curving horned moustache.

He or an associate would carry a large feed sack in which to stuff bad boys and carry them away—usually no farther than a snowbank in the vicinity. Another sack or basket would hold gifts for those who had been good.

Unlike his gentler counterpart, he rarely deigned to ask if he could come in but stormed into the house like an avenging demon, rattling his chain, shaking his bells, and making fierce noises no one could understand. Bad boys would cringe in terror, but there was no refuge for them. Custom dictated that even brothers or sisters would propel the erring ones forward to be punished with voice, switch, or lash.

Every child knew he'd be coming and awaited his arrival with a curious mixture of eagerness, dread, and outright terror. On Christmas Eve, they knew his onslaught was imminent by the sound of his bells, the rattling of twigs across the window, a rude knock, and the thumping of his booted feet on the stairs.

In remote villages the *Belsnickel* would sometimes attract

children by slamming open the front door. He would throw handfuls of nuts and candy on the floor, and then after children scrambled after his bait, he'd pounce upon them, wielding whip and sticks right and left indiscriminately, on the basic premise that the unrighteous deserved it and the righteous weren't as righteous as people thought they were.

The institution of the *Belsnickel* and *Christkindel* survived for about 150 years in America. But as German descendants assimilated into America's mainstream, gradually old country traditions began to die out.

SINTERKLAAS/SANTA CLAUS

Henry Hudson was in the service of the Dutch East India Company when his ship, the *Half Moon*, first entered what later became known as the Hudson River in 1609. By 1623, the Dutch formally decreed that the entire region—land between latitudes 40 and 45 degrees—be organized into the province of New Netherland. In May of 1624, thirty families, mostly Walloon (Celtic people from the Low Countries), reached Manhattan Island, where most of them decided to put down roots. The rest stayed on the ship and later disembarked upriver at Fort Orange (which grew into Albany). Within a year, three more shiploads of colonists arrived. Governor Peter Minuit arrived in 1626 and bought Manhattan Island from the Iroquois for a reputed twenty-four dollars' worth of beads. Fort Amsterdam was erected on its lower end. The first church was dedicated to *Sinterklaas* (meaning, of course, Holy Nicholas). Later on, under the peg-legged governor, Peter Stuyvesant, the colony's population increased from two thousand to ten thousand.

But in 1664, England's King Charles II, alarmed at the Dutch presence in America, sent four warships, manned with 125 guns and 500 fighting men, to terminate that presence. Since the Dutch were unprepared for such military might, they peaceably surrendered; consequently, they were permitted to remain on the land they loved, and so New Amsterdam became New York. But the very heart and soul remained Dutch—and always, deep down, St. Nicholas has remained its patron saint. Nevertheless, as time passed and immigrants from many nations settled in the colony, memories of *Sinterklaas* grew dim.

COINCIDENCE—OR FATE?

By now, in the ongoing soap opera of St. Nicholas, we've learned that just when it appears certain circumstances have cornered him in a box canyon, and his doom is certain, something totally unexpected takes place, and he is rescued once again. And so it happens now: enter Washington Irving (1783–1859).

Since Irving, having been born to wealthy Scotch-Irish parents, did not have to work, he made little effort to do so, much preferring the life of a dilettante, devouring literature and embarking on a Grand Tour of Europe. Chances are, none of us would ever have heard of him had it not been for a rather quirky intervention of fate.

Lawrence Wheeler, my esteemed late father, articulated a truth in these pithy words: "No one is ever completely useless—you can always serve as a horrible example." Apparently, such a horrible example was Samuel Latham Mitchell's ponderous, pretentious, and undeniably boring guidebook *The Picture of New York*. Being both young and impatient with pretense, Washington Irving and his brother Peter decided to write a satire based on Mitchell's unfortunate brainchild.

But to their dismay, the manuscript kept growing bigger and bigger. When Peter gave up on it and wandered off to Europe, the younger brother, being left to carry on alone the best he could, found the subject so fascinating he burrowed deeply into New Amsterdam history and didn't emerge until he'd created a seven-volume mock epic, pretentiously titled *A History of New York from the Beginning of the World to the End of the Dutch Dynasty*. He attributed the monstrosity to one Diedrich Knickerbocker. According to William Bennett, "The surname *Knickerbocker* was a popular term for New Yorkers of Dutch ancestry."[1] Though, on the surface, it appeared to be little more than an irreverent spoof, it was in reality a literary and historical tour de force, the result of both wide reading in the classics and prodigious research. The literary world, on both sides of the Atlantic, laughed it (and Irving) into an overnight success.

As fate would have it, Irving's brother-in-law, John Pintard, father of the New York Historical Society, had given him the suggestion that he incorporate St. Nicholas into the mock epic; which he did. The following is an example:

> And the sage Oloffe dreamed a dream—and lo, the good St. Nicholas came riding over the tops of the trees, in that self same wagon wherein he brings his yearly presents to children, and he descended hard by where the heroes of Communipaw had made their late repast. And he lit his pipe by the fire, and sat himself down and smoked; and as he smoked the smoke from his pipe ascended into the air and spread like a cloud overhead. And Oloffe bethought him, and he hastened and climbed up to the top of one of the tallest trees, and saw that the smoke spread over a great extent of country—and as he considered it more attentively, he fancied that the great volume of smoke assumed a variety of marvelous forms, where in dim obscurity he saw shadowed out palaces and domes and lofty spires, all of which lasted but a moment, and then faded away, until the whole rolled off, and nothing but the green woods were left. And when St. Nicholas had smoked his pipe, he twisted it in his hat-band, and laying his finger beside his nose, gave the astonished Van Kortlandt a very significant look, then mounting his wagon, he returned over the tree-tops and disappeared.[2]

Historian Charles Jones maintains that without Irving there would be no Santa Claus. The epic contains two dozen references to St. Nicholas, and resulted in the overnight popularity of St. Nicholas in America, especially among the literati.[3]

THE NIGHT BEFORE CHRISTMAS

Enter Clement Clark Moore (1779–1863), who, like Irving, was born to wealth. The son of the second Episcopal bishop of New York and onetime president of Columbia University, Dr. Moore had been willed the Chelsea section of New York sweeping from Ninth Avenue to the river from his father-in-law, Captain Thomas Clark. Dr. Moore, one of the founders of the New York Theological Seminary, not only served as a pro bono professor there, but was also well-known as a Hebrew and Greek scholar.

William Armstrong, in an insightful 1917 tribute to Moore, wrote:

Nearly a century ago, the section still known to New York as Chelsea was a vast estate with tree-shaded lawns and a great mansion, the home to Dr. Moore. There he wrote "The Night Before Christmas," for his little daughters, in honor of the [1822] season. And on Christmas Eve he read it to them in surroundings ideally suited to such a poem: the great, ever-green-decked room, illumined by the glow of candles and of a yule log blazing in a cavernous fireplace. One can fancy those little girls listening in awed delight as they stole glances toward the fireplace, wondering whether Santa Claus might not be even then on the brink of dropping in.

The legend of "The Night Before Christmas" had been told to Dr. Moore in his boyhood by a Dutch settler, then laboring in green fields that now are busy New York streets; a man who in his fat jollity is said to have resembled strongly Santa Claus himself. The whole history of the poem is, indeed, one of pure joyousness throughout, inspired by happy memories, written from love for little ones, and spreading in its instant appeal throughout the world from the moment when it first appeared in print, unknown to the good doctor, who was more surprised than any as to how it got there. About this last fact, though, there lingers no puzzling mystery. The daughter of a clerical friend, Miss Butler, visiting the Moore home, copied the poem from an album and took it back home with her. One year later, the Troy *Sentinel*, on December 23, 1823, gave it as a Christmas present to the world.

Armstrong goes on to point out that it is almost ironic that the ponderous Hebrew dictionary on which Moore thought to anchor his frame is unknown today, but "the poem that he deemed a trifling thing outweighed in richness all his more ambitious strivings, because it touched a Christmas spark in every human heart."

Armstrong notes that the poem "seems to have well reflected its writer's genial love of healthful laughter, his kindly heart, his rare gentleness." The poem was his gift to the world: not a penny in royalties would Dr. Moore accept.

Movingly, Armstrong sums up Moore's life in these words:

Indeed, the entire life of Dr. Moore was marked by disregard for material things he might have chosen had he not preferred the simpler ones. But surely otherwise he could not have spoken so unerringly to children's hearts. Had he willed it, his name might stand today in the list of dead and gone landed magnates of New York. He chose, instead, to live to help and inspire others. All the year around his life seems to have kept Christmas, for his was a spirit that loved to give.[4]

Originally, the poem was called "A Visit from St. Nicholas;" however, many know it today as "The Night Before Christmas."

"A VISIT FROM ST. NICHOLAS"

Twas the night before Christmas when all through the house
Not a creature was stirring, not even a mouse;
The stockings were hung by the chimney with care,
In hopes that St. Nicholas soon would be there;
The children were nestled all snug in their beds,
While visions of sugar-plums danced through their heads;
And Mama in her kerchief, and I in my cap,
Had just settled our brains for a long winter's nap—
When out on the lawn there rose such a clatter,
I sprang from my bed to see what was the matter.
Away to the window I flew like a flash.

Tore open the shutters and threw up the sash.

The moon, on the breast of the new-fallen snow,

Gave a luster of mid-day to objects below,

When, what to my wondering eyes should appear

But a miniature sleigh, and eight tiny reindeer,

With a little old driver, so lively and quick,

I knew in a moment it must be St. Nick.

More rapid than eagles his coursers they came,

And he whistled, and shouted, and called them by name:

"Now, Dasher! now, Dancer, now, Prancer and Vixen!

On, Comet! on, Cupid! on, Donder and Blitzen—

To the top of the porch, to the top of the wall!

Now, dash away, dash away, dash away all!"

As leaves before the wild hurricane fly,

When they meet with an obstacle, mount to the sky,

So, up to the house top the coursers they flew,

With a sleigh full of toys—and St. Nicholas, too.

And then in a twinkling I heard on the roof,

The prancing and pawing of each little hoof.

As I drew in my head, and was turning around,

Down the chimney St. Nicholas came with a bound.

He was dressed all in fur from his head to his foot,

And his clothes were all tarnished with ashes and soot;

A bundle of toys he had flung on his back.

And he looked like a peddler just opening his pack.

His eyes how they twinkled! his dimples how merry!

His cheeks were like roses, his nose like a cherry;

His droll little mouth was drawn up like a bow,

And the beard on his chin was as white as the snow.

The stump of a pipe he held tight in his teeth,

And the smoke, it encircled his head like a wreath.

He had a broad face, and a little round belly,

That shook when he laughed, like a bowl full of jelly.

He was chubby and plump—a right jolly old elf;

And I laughed when I saw him, in spite of myself.

A wink of his eye, and a twist of his head,

Soon gave me to know I had nothing to dread.

He spoke not a word, but went straight to his work,

And filled all the stockings; then turned with a jerk,

And laying his finger aside of his nose,

And giving a nod, up the chimney he rose.

He sprang to his sleigh, to his team gave a whistle,

And away they all flew like the down of a thistle;

But I heard him exclaim, ere he drove out of sight,

"HAPPY CHRISTMAS TO ALL AND TO ALL A GOOD
NIGHT!"[5]

It would be twenty-two years before the erudite Dr. Moore would admit publicly that he'd written the poem. It may well have been reprinted more than any other poem ever written. Clearly, it is based on Irving's *Knickerbocker* imagery, except that Moore miniaturized him to elf size. Author Mark Arnest maintains that "more than anything else, 'The Night Before Christmas' changed the public perception of Christmas—and its mention of St. Nicholas leaving gifts for children was particularly influential." Also, "it turned the public celebration inward toward the family. A child-centered celebration was new in the United States."[6]

And author Stephen Nissenbaum maintains that, inadvertent though it may have been, Moore permanently altered the public's perception of St. Nicholas. He did so by stripping the saint of his authority, his dignity, even his very identity as a bishop—not only defrocked, but *declassed* him as well.[7]

We owe a real debt to Nissenbaum, for he provides us with the very moment in American Christmas history when the traditional St. Nicholas, for all practical purposes, ceased to exist this side of the Atlantic. From this moment on, we must regard Santa Claus as a uniquely American construct almost totally divorced from religion.

But not yet was the persona of Santa Claus set in stone.

THOMAS NAST

Next on the scene was Thomas Nast (1840–1902), one of thousands of German immigrants pouring into the city of New York. He would learn English in school, where whatever gifts anyone received at Christmas tended to come in the name of Santa Claus. By now the name St. Nicholas was being used less and less.

It was the Golden Age of Print and also the Golden Age of Harper, the world's then preeminent publishing house. In 1862, the twenty-two-year-old Nast joined *Harper's Weekly* as a staff illustrator.

America's Civil War was raging, and the fortunes of President Lincoln and the Union appeared mighty bleak that winter of 1862. In an attempt to bring hope to the magazine's readers, Nash sketched out a frontispiece in which Santa, robed in the Stars and Stripes, was depicted as distributing presents from his reindeer-pulled sleigh to the cheering Union soldiers. So popular was it that *Harper's* editors told him to keep those Santa Claus woodcuts coming, which he did. After the war, many ex-Confederate troops reportedly admitted that those were some of the most demoralizing moments in the entire conflict: seeing Santa side with the North in the Nast portrayals. Lincoln maintained that Nast was his best recruiting agent.

After the war, the public insisted that those yearly Santa Claus woodcuts continue to hold center stage in *Harper's*. During that time, Nast also became the nation's most famous political cartoonist, almost single-handedly destroying New York's infamous Tammany Hall and also creating the Republican elephant and Democratic donkey icons.

During the quarter century (1862–1888) of Nast's Santa Claus woodcuts, Santa evolved some more: from small and gnomelike into the furry *Belznickel* look and finally into rotundity, leading many readers to wonder how Santa managed to squeeze all that corpulence into—and out of—fireplace shafts. Nast also made him more overtly kind and approachable. And by the 1870s, Christmas cards with Nast's Santa images began to be sold all across America and Europe. Thus, by the time Nast turned in his last submission in 1886, he'd hammered his personal perception of what Santa Claus looked like and acted like into the American psyche for all time—and, for good measure, helped make Santa the chief pitchman for the Christmas shopping season. Significantly, Nast could have preserved at least part of his spiritual persona had he so desired, but he did not.

ENTER VIRGINIA

The most widely publicized and circulated editorial of all time was written anonymously by Frances Pharcellus Church and was published by the *New York Sun* on September 21, 1897. An eight-year-old girl, Virginia O'Hanlon, who had always believed in the existence of Santa Claus (that is, St. Nicholas), found her beliefs challenged by children she knew. When even her father's answers seemed evasive, she turned to the family court of last resort: the *Sun* Question and Answer column, for Father had always said, "If you see it in the *Sun*, it's so."

Her letter to the editor, after giving her age, posed this question:

> Some of my little friends say there is no Santa Claus. Papa says, "If you see it in the *Sun*, it's so." Please tell me the truth, is there a Santa Claus?—Virginia O'Hanlon

As day after day passed and Virginia saw no answer to her letter in the Question and Answer column, she grew more and more disconsolate. But one day Dr. O'Hanlon called his daughter from his downtown office—a *big* event, for telephones were then used only for emergencies or major news—and told her, "Virginia, they *did* answer your letter. They gave you a whole editorial!"

The editorial was titled "YES, VIRGINIA, THERE IS A SANTA CLAUS!" and read as follows:

> We take pleasure in answering at once and thus prominently the communication below, expressing at the same time our great satisfaction that its faithful author is numbered among the friends of the *Sun*.

After giving the text of the girl's letter, the editorial continued:

> Virginia, your little friends are wrong. They have been affected by the skepticism of a skeptical age. They do not believe except they see. They think that nothing can be which is not comprehensible by their little minds.
>
> All minds, Virginia, whether they be men's or children's, are little. In this great universe of ours man is a mere insect, an ant, in his intellect, as compared with the boundless world about him, as measured by the intelligence capable of grasping the whole of truth and knowledge.
>
> Yes, Virginia, there is a Santa Claus. He exists as certainly as love and generosity and devotion exist, and you

know that they abound and give to your life its highest beauty and joy. Alas! How dreary would be the world if there were no Santa Claus! It would be dreary as if there were no Virginias.

There would be no childlike faith then, no poetry, no romance to make tolerable this existence. We should have no enjoyment except in sense and sight. The eternal light with which childhood fills the world would be extinguished.

Not believe in Santa Claus! You might as well not believe in fairies! You might get your papa to hire men to watch in all the chimneys on Christmas Eve to catch Santa Claus, but even if they did not see Santa Claus coming down, what would that prove?

Nobody sees Santa Claus, but that is no sign that there is no Santa Claus. The most real things in the world are those that neither children nor men can see. Did you ever see fairies dancing on the lawn? Of course not, but that's no proof that they are not there. Nobody can conceive or imagine all the wonders that are unseen and unseeable in the world.

You tear apart a baby's rattle and see what makes the noise inside, but there is a veil covering the unseen world which not the strongest man, nor even the united strength of all the strongest men that ever lived, could tear apart.

Only faith, fancy, poetry, love, romance, can push aside that curtain and view and picture the supernatural beauty and glory beyond. Is it all real? Ah, Virginia, in all this world there is nothing else real and abiding.

No Santa Claus! Thank God he lives, and he lives

forever. A thousand years from now, Virginia, nay, ten times ten thousand years from now, he will continue to make glad the heart of childhood.[8]

Ironically, Mr. Church had initially been anything but happy about being given the assignment of responding to Virginia's letter, for he was known as being a cynical, crusty fellow, had been a Civil War correspondent, and had no children of his own. Nevertheless, he penned this remarkable editorial. The editorial went *everywhere*, and did much to validate the place of Santa Claus/St. Nicholas in American culture.[9]

. . . AND NORMAN ROCKWELL

Artist Norman Rockwell (1894–1978) dominated his age more than any other artist. The cover of the *Saturday Evening Post* was his showcase for more than forty years, giving him an audience larger than any other artist in history, with three hundred covers in all. Over the years, Rockwell's depictions of Santa Claus were spread out through a number of magazines, Hallmark Christmas cards, and advertisements. Of the ten that graced the covers of the *Post*, the most famous and talked-about Christmas cover ever was *The Discovery*, depicting a little boy rummaging around in his parents' chest of drawers, at the very moment he discovered his father's Santa Claus suit and beard. That look of absolute shock, disbelief, and betrayal has never been recaptured by any other artist.[10]

SUNDBLOM AND COCA-COLA; AND RUDOLPH

Haddon Hubbard Sundblom (1899–1976) picked up where Rockwell left off. For twenty years, his memorable ad paintings depicting Santa Claus, always in the vicinity of a bottle of Coca-Cola, held center stage on back covers of the nation's leading magazines. By the time Sundblom was through, only one thing was lacking; and that contribution was made by Robert L. May for the advertising department of Montgomery Ward in 1939. His story of Rudolph, the Red-Nosed Reindeer was used as a giveaway that Christmas. Millions were picked up. Then Gene Autry and Bing Crosby made the Phi Bete Johnny Marks song a worldwide best seller, moving more than fifty million copies.

With that, the lid was nailed down on the persona of Santa Claus.

10

SAINT NICHOLAS TODAY

Now—finally—we arrive at our own time. It is interesting to trace what is the same, and what has changed, since Washington Irving, Thomas Nast, Clement Moore, Norman Rockwell, and Haddon Sundblom on this side of the Atlantic, as well as the rest of the world.

THE ORTHODOX WORLD

A good place to start would be Beit Jala in Palestine or Demre, Turkey, and experience the East that gave birth to St. Nicholas. In the Muslim world, St. Nicholas is known and revered, but he is not a central figure to them. The Turks call him *Noel Baba* and are proud of him. Increasingly, they are realizing that he represents a potential gold mine in twenty-first-century tourism as an icon, as a bridge between East and West, and as a magnet for world peace.

The St. Nicholas Church of Myra (Demre now) has been partially restored. An Orthodox liturgy is offered in the church, which is attended by an ecumenical and interfaith gathering there early each December. The sarcophagus that once contained St. Nicholas's body can still be seen in one of the side chapels, as can iconlike murals. A great statue of Santa Claus has been erected in the garden, indicating a call for peace to the children of the world.

Without question, St. Nicholas's greatest bastion remains what it has always been—the far-flung world of Orthodox Christianity. Even though Turkey is today predominantly Muslim, the nominal head of Orthodox Christianity remains the patriarch of Constantinople (Istanbul). For most of the twentieth century, it appeared the largest number of Orthodox Christianity believers in the world had been disenfranchised, but when Communism fell, once again it became apparent that Orthodox Christianity remained alive and well in Russia, and St. Nicholas remained the most popular saint in all Russia. In fact, it appears that almost every church in Russia has at least one St. Nicholas icon.

Should you wish to get a feel for what St. Nicholas means to Eastern Orthodoxy, all you have to do is check to see if your nearest Eastern (or Greek or Russian) Orthodox church has services on December 5, St. Nicholas Eve. Chances are they will. You will note that the faithful will leave their shoes outside the church door; upon leaving the services each will find gold coins (actually chocolates wrapped in gold foil) in them, symbolizing the gold dowries for the three dowerless sisters. During the services you will see St. Nicholas appear in his traditional bishop's garb.

One of the great hidden St. Nicholas treasures is his cave at the Greek Orthodox Church in Beit Jala. This war-torn and somewhat neglected church resounds with the echoes of praise from the thousands of pilgrims who gather here for the annual St. Nicholas festival. Beneath the main cave is the cave where St. Nicholas is said to have lived during his time in the Holy Land.

But what may surprise you most will be St. Nicholas's place in the spiritual life of Orthodox Christians. He is honored twice: both on December 6 and on May 9, celebrating both the ancient Rosalia festival and the removal of his bones to Bari. Interestingly enough, in both Orthodox and Anglican/Episcopal churches, St. Nicholas is revered most, not for his gift-bringing, but for being the ultimate pastor, the ultimate shepherd, second in that respect only to Christ Himself.

Perhaps it is because of this pastoral dimension that Orthodox Christianity, in its weekly liturgical cycle, singles out three human beings by name: Mary, the mother of Christ; John, the Forerunner; and St. Nicholas.

BARI, ITALY

Because of St. Nicholas's presence here, Bari has become one of Europe's greatest ecumenical centers. Case in point: an Orthodox chapel can be found inside the Roman Catholic basilica. Here Christians from many different denominations come each May for symposiums, worship, and, of course, the annual celebration commemorating the translation of the relics of St. Nicholas of Myra to Bari in 1087. During this remembrance an image of St. Nicholas is taken from the Orthodox church and carried in procession down to the port. There it is placed in a boat and carried out into deeper water. It is returned during an unforgettable night procession. Several days of celebration follow. In the basilica, after a solemn mass, the prior (in the presence of the archbishop of Bari) withdraws the "Holy Manna" that has accumulated in the crypt during the year. This manna is then poured into hand-painted bottles and made available to pilgrims (for a hefty price). Another integral part of the annual celebration is the sailing of a replica of the ship *Caravella* that brought the St. Nicholas relics here nine centuries ago.

THE DUTCH WORLD

We turn to the Netherlands next, for they have celebrated St. Nicholas for close to a thousand years (there were more than twenty St. Nicholas churches as early as the twelfth and thirteenth centuries). What is called *Oude Kerk in Oude Kerkplein* (Old Church on Old Church Square) in Amsterdam was consecrated to St. Nicholas back in 1325. So total was their devotion to the saint that people in those days often called the citizens of Amsterdam *Sinter Klassmannen*.

Early in November (even earlier for many Dutch shop-keepers), St. Nicholas begins to make his presence felt. Shop windows begin to fill up with St. Nicholas goodies and memorabilia—gift-wrapped cardboard boxes, replicas of St. Nicholas and Black Pete, chocolate letters, *pepernoten* (small, round, hard cookies made with seasonal spices), and a host of related things. With each day that passes, the anticipation of the children continues to build.

Toward the latter part of November, there comes an event that even today brings virtually the entire nation to a halt: the arrival of St. Nicholas and his Black Pete contingent from Spain. Amsterdam has long held the honor of welcoming them first, and the ship invariably bears the name *Spanje* (Spain). At the same time, there are similar arrivals all over the nation: some by boat, some by jet, some by helicopter, some by conveyances such as trolleys, carriages, trains, bicycles—even taxis.

In Amsterdam, the steamer docks amid the sounds of church bells, cheering crowds, and booming guns. Hundreds of thousands of Amsterdamers crowd the streets. Creeds mean little on this day, for St. Nicholas has become a universally beloved ecumenical figure. Now the stately saint descends from the ship and mounts his great white horse. Invariably, his beard will be long and white, and he wears gloves, a white robe, a crimson mantle, and a tall, red mitre headdress. In his hand he carries a golden crosier, a staff shaped like a shepherd's crook.

Along the way, it is clear that the saint enjoys being in the company of the children, each of them craning their necks for a glimpse of him. Most fortunate are those perched on the shoulders of an adult, thus gaining a better view. *Sinterklaas* is profoundly obliging. He never hesitates to stop and tweak a miniature nose or grasp a small outstretched hand along the way. *Sinterklaas* may possibly stop to remind some children about their conduct records, which he has been keeping in his Big Red Book. He often reads from this carefully recorded log when out among his juvenile followers. It reveals his intimate knowledge of their year's activities, good and bad.[1]

Some of the children rush toward him (especially when he descends from his horse and is walking among them); others, however, shyly hold back, clearly awed by the immortal bishop. As he speaks with them, he is likely to drop hints about what kind of tidbits his horse likes best. The children know exactly what he's talking about, for each of them will leave such a snack in a shoe near the hearth at home, in hopes that St. Nicholas will come during the night and leave a treat behind—if they have been good, of course.

The children are everywhere and have been waiting for what seems an eternity to them. Many of them don paper bishop's mitres bought in costume shops as they prepare to greet their saint. As the procession moves away from the ancient St. Nicholas Church, little else can move on the snarled streets. While St. Nicholas waves, the brigade of Black Petes ham it up: they dance; they ride funny little motor scooters; they tell jokes and pass out sweets to each of the children within reach.

Black Pete couldn't be more of a contrast to St. Nicholas. He and his fellows are usually dressed like medieval Spanish pages, complete with "long stockings, short, puffed britches, tight-fitting jacket, pleated collar, and plumed beret tipped over one ear. All are in bright contrasting colors."[2]

Pete carries with him certain standard props. The most important—and dreaded—is the famous Big Red Book in which *Sinterklaas* keeps those all-important records of the children's behavior. Pete lets them know that keeping those records is a full-time job for him and the saint back in sunny Spain. Pete is also likely to carry a handful of birch rods or switches. The switches are enough to keep the children on their best behavior. Bad children may receive no treats at all, only the rod or a switch. But the third prop is everyone's favorite: the big sack filled with goodies. Continually, he tosses cookies, fruits (the children love oranges), chocolates, and other sweets, especially *pepernoten*. Pete enjoys engaging with foolery with the children. Often he will not only join them in singing and dancing but will lead them in a chorus. He is always available to introduce a willing youngster to the famed *Sinterklaas* or to tousle a nearby head of hair. Tots and teens alike delight in his tricks and silly actions. Consequently, wherever Pete is found, there will inevitably be a group of young people surrounding him.[3]

Everyone tries to get in on the act: civic officials, brass bands, acrobats, entertainers, children's organizations, floats, and police motorcades throng the streets in the wake of St.

Nicholas. In Amsterdam, the parade often winds its way clear to the Royal Palace, where, in all likelihood, the queen will be waiting. The lack of support of Dutch Protestant leaders for all this has had a predictable result: every year the crowds are larger than those of the previous year.

The days and nights that follow are busy ones for all the St. Nicholases and Black Petes, for the genius of the Dutch St. Nicholas season is that the two principals are tightly woven into the very fabric of their Christmas season, much more so than is true with Santa Claus in America. At nighttime it is assumed that they are riding across Holland's rooftops, listening in at chimneys to verify their suppositions as to children's behavior. Pete supposedly slides down each chimney (or otherwise gains admittance to the house) in order to exchange small gifts for the hay or carrots left in the children's shoes for the horse. During daylight hours they are even busier: visiting classrooms, hospitals, department stores, restaurants, offices, and innumerable private homes. There are parades to ride in, additional gifts to distribute, enthusiastic but sometimes off-key singing to listen to, confessions to hear, admonitions to give. Hardly a minute can they count their own.[4]

Without question, over the thousand years that the Dutch have celebrated St. Nicholas, they have structured and finessed the annual season of Nicholastide to the point where it would be difficult to improve on it. For this reason, Christmasaholics from all over the world make a point of traveling to the Netherlands in order to take part in the annual St. Nicholas festivities.

ALSACE-LORRAINE, FRANCE

St. Nicholas is as beloved in Lorraine as he is in Holland, and his appearances there are similar to those in the Netherlands. When the children see him coming down the street in his crimson bishop's robe and pointed miter, they cheer and clap. But they tend to recoil in fear when they see St. Nicholas's inseparable companion, *Pere Fouetard*. Like *Zwarte Piet*, he carries a bundle of switches with him. And he appears to have an uncomfortably accurate memory, remembering which boys and girls misbehaved during the past twelve months. Now and then he will playfully whack certain children's toes as they pass.

In some places in Lorraine, a standard feature of the procession will be a cart carrying a salt barrel. Sticking out at the top are three naked boys, the iconic symbol of the Three Children in the Salt Tub legend.[5]

Just as is true in the Netherlands, the gifts children receive are given in the name of St. Nicholas. Shoes, stockings, or baskets left by the fireplace on the Eve of St. Nicholas are found filled the morning of December 6 with sweets, gingerbread figures, and fruit. Carrots and hay are left for St. Nicholas's horse, or donkey, a glass of wine for the saint. In Lorraine, on December 4, children intently watch the sky: if it is red, it means that St. Nicholas is busy cooking the cakes he'll be delivering the next night. St. Nicholas is also extremely popular in Alsace.[6]

Today, the Church of Nicolas de Port in Lorraine is one of

the grandest such churches in the world. Its history goes back to St. Nicholas Day, 1244.

In much of France today, *Pere Noel*, a St. Nicholas surrogate, rules over the Christmas season. Like St. Nicholas, *Pere Noel* is tall, thin, has a white beard, and wears a long red robe. On his back, he often carries a sack of treats and toys for the children. Sometimes a donkey carries that sack for him. Antique dealers offer dozens of Bishop Nicholas tinted postcards created in France. *Pere Noel* is a strange amalgamation of both St. Nicholas and Santa Claus in that he brings small gifts and candy treats to children both on December 6 and on Christmas Eve. Like Santa Claus, supposedly *Pere Noel* lives at the North Pole. *Pere Noel* has a helper too, *Pere Fouetard* (Father Whipper), who informs his master which children have not behaved; however, *Pere Fouetard* is not nearly as visible in France as Black Pete is in the Netherlands. Many children put their shoes near the fireplace, crèche, or Christmas tree on Christmas Eve, hoping that *Pere Noel* will leave presents in them. The children open their presents on Christmas Day, the adults on New Year's Day.[7]

BELGIUM/FLANDERS

Since Flanders has, throughout history, been so closely associated with Holland, it should come as no surprise to discover that St. Nicholas is deeply revered here. The city of Sint Niklaas has a St. Nicholas church, outside of which has been erected an enormous image of St. Nicholas and the three children in a barrel. St. Nicholas is even part of the official city seal and street decor. The people of Sint Niklaas have their own unique way of greeting the arrival of St. Nicholas and *Zwarte Piet*. A weekend family celebration in the style of a circus is held, and St. Nicholas presides from a throne with his helpers. Several times during weekend performances, he directly addresses the children.

The people of Flanders have an ongoing battle with the intrusion of the Americanized Santa Claus. Staged arrests of Santa Claus are sometimes held on their streets, and Santa Claus is forbidden to appear before December 7.

LUXEMBOURG

On the Sunday preceding the December festival of St. Nicholas, the Grand Duchy of Luxembourg welcomes the saint in its cities, towns, and villages. In some places, such as in Echternacht, St. Nicholas and his companion, *Hoêsecker*, arrive by boat. Waiting for them on the shore will be the town mayor, resplendent in his robes, as well as the aldermen by his side. These officials escort their distinguished visitors to town in a horse-drawn carriage. A large procession follows, including a local band that makes a great deal of noise.

In the town itself a throng of children shout, hop, and jump excitedly as Nicholas and *Hoêsecker* make their triumphant approach to the old Town Hall in the marketplace. The band plays all the songs the boys and girls know. The children dread *Hoêsecker* as much as they love Nicholas. Like *Pere Fouetard*, *Hoêsecker* carries switches on his back, and he never hesitates to whip a lazy or disobedient child. At the ceremonies in the marketplace, each one receives a big paper bag bulging with apples, cakes, and bonbons. The little ones in their mothers' arms get their presents first, then the children up to twelve. Meanwhile the band strikes up one lively Christmas tune after another.[8]

AUSTRIA AND GERMANY

St. Nicholas is still very popular in both south Germany and Austria. In Austria, *Krampus*, one of the more frightening assistants of St. Nicholas, terrifies many of the children. Reports of near-violent attacks by this assistant does little to enhance the public perception of the saint. St. Nicholas is found shaped into breads, candies, and almost every other imaginable food in Austria. Christmas markets in Salzburg and Vienna have vast arrays of St. Nicholas items to delight the shoppers.

UNITED KINGDOM

St. Nicholas has long been beloved in Britain. In fact, there are almost five hundred churches dedicated to St. Nicholas here, more than four hundred in England alone. The most famous of them is probably King's College chapel in Cambridge. This splendid chapel is known the world over for its great medieval stained-glass depictions of St. Nicholas and its annual Festival of Nine Lessons and Carols on its Christmas Eve broadcast around the world. In Aberdeen, Scotland, there can be found the Kirk of St. Nicholas, which is both Congregational and Presbyterian Church of Scotland. Just about a mile from it, in the St. Margaret of Scotland Episcopal Church, can be found one of the most exquisite Comper chapels of St. Nicholas in the world, designed by Sir John Ninian Comper (1864–1960), a great Gothic Revival architect. One of England's most famous churches is St. Nicholas Church of Durham, and another is St. Nicholas Cathedral in Newcastle upon Tyne.

Famed British composer Benjamin Britten composed a cantata for St. Nicholas that is performed every year in concerts and Advent services throughout Britain. Today, Anglican leaders have begun a strong movement to bring back St. Nicholas and the spiritual dimension of Christmas in order to counter the secularizing effects of Father Christmas. All too often today, it is the pagan antecedents of Christianity, with their winter solstice connections, that are popularized by the media.

THE UNITED STATES

Without question, Santa Claus is the most pervasive Christmas presence in America today. He is the force that propels the nation's most lucrative selling season, and he appears in malls all across the country, where long lines of children climb up on his knee and tell him what they want for Christmas. He has become a staple of secular Christmas music.

Santa has also been incorporated into the celebrations of churchgoers. Often a family member dresses up in a Santa Claus suit to add an extra dimension to the distribution of presents. Santas ring Salvation Army bells as they encourage shoppers to help the needy and destitute. Many of those who wear Santa suits are involved in admirable philanthropic causes, seeking to make a real difference in their communities.

But having said this, I am convicted that Santa Claus's once almost total dominance over the American Christmas season is today being challenged. More and more people are openly questioning why the conspicuous-consumption Santa persona should continue to be considered the face of what once was a sacred season. I believe our current economic recession is already accelerating this shift toward the original spiritual persona of St. Nicholas. For during flush times, we feel self-sufficient; during tough times, we turn to a Higher Power for help.

THE REST OF THE WORLD

Although Christmas is universally celebrated in ostensibly Christian nations, because of the ubiquitousness of mass media today, there is hardly a culture on the planet that has not come to terms with the holiday—whether to accept the almost totally secular persona of Santa Claus or to search for a spiritual persona such as the original bishop of Myra.

OUR LAST ST. NICHOLAS STORY

We have shared together most of the significant St. Nicholas stories, down through the ages. We began with certifiably true ones. But as time passed, miraculous elements became almost staples in the genre. After the Renaissance, more and more they tended to become ever more secular. But one constant remains: none of them have been works of art. None but this last one.

I stumbled on it by chance a number of years ago, and have never been able to reread it without being deeply moved. It is truly one of a kind. It fills in the last missing piece of our mosaic of Christmas stories—a mighty big piece, I might add: St. Nicholas's influence in the Russian Orthodox church. For eleven hundred years now, farther back than is true for even the Netherlands, St. Nicholas has reigned supreme in Russian churches, except during the Bolshevik/Communism years. During the second decade of the twentieth century, Czar Nicholas II became the fall guy for those horrendous casualties against the Japanese and then Russian troops. Bolshevik mastermind Vladimir Lenin capitalized on that instability by turning Russia into a police state. It appeared to the world that Christianity in Russia was all but dead. Yet, deep in the very soul of Russians it stubbornly refused to die—it just went underground, along with its patron saint, Nicholas. So it was that when the Berlin Wall fell and the Soviet dominoes began to topple across Eastern Europe, and Communism was discredited, the Russian Orthodox Church and St. Nicholas sprang back as though there'd never been a hiatus at all. And even with losing 25 percent of its land mass to breakaway republics, Russia is still, by far, the world's largest nation, stretching across eight time zones, all the way from Norway to Alaska. Furthermore, both the church and St. Nicholas are also alive and well in the breakaway republics.

All this complexity is mirrored in this greatest of all St. Nicholas stories, Meriel Buchanan's "The Miracle of St. Nicholas,"[9] written in 1919, while Russia was in chaos after WWI and the fall of the Romanov dynasty. It takes the reader through World War I, the terrible casualties, the collapse of the Romanov government, the chaos that followed, the triumph of Bolshevism, and the apparent defeat of Christianity and St. Nicholas in Russia. Yet Buchanan's riveting conclusion implies that both Christianity and St. Nicholas will somehow, sometime, come back. They did—it just took seventy long years.

THE MIRACLE OF ST. NICHOLAS

The trees on the opposite shore made a soft line of shadow against the sky of palest, palest gold. Not a ripple stirred the still surface of the river, not a breath of wind rustled in the grass along the banks. Drifting in a pearly, soft haze a little boat moved like a silent spirit across the water. From the village, hidden amidst the trees, came a distant murmur of voices, now and then a snatch of song that broke off as if the singer had suddenly been reminded that his time for singing would perhaps be short.

But the boy and the girl who sat alone by the river were silent, the girl's head lying on the boy's shoulder, his cheek resting on her soft, dark hair. Barely a week ago they had been married in the old wooden church whose star-painted dome showed above the ghostly trees. They had looked forward to years of peace and happiness—and now tomorrow the boy, with the rest of the men of the village, was leaving to fight the Germans.

So they sat by the river and looked across into the sunset and found no words to say to each other, their hearts too full of troubled fears and pain that could find no expression in speech. There was nothing to do, the decree had gone forth, and dumbly they submitted to it. Kolia must go and be a soldier, and Praskovia, the child-wife, must wait till he came back, and pray for him every day, and once a week burn a candle for him before the icon of St. Nicholas, his patron saint. That was all there was to tell, so what was the use of talking as they sat by the river clinging to each other as if somehow they thought that by sitting very close they could fill the loneliness that would be theirs tomorrow with the dear memory of the touch of hands and lips? And Time, relentless and inexorable, counted the minutes one by one, and drew the soft gray veil of the summer night over the world's poor tortured face.

≈

Summer passed and the trees along the banks of the river turned to flaming gold and crimson till the water seemed on fire with their reflected glory under the soft blue haze of the autumn sky. And presently the leaves began to fall and the bare branches whispered and rustled as if spirits moved among them and shook them to sudden sighs and laughter. And gray under the grayness of the sky the broad river lay sullen and dark, while little black tugs churned up and down dragging heavy barges laden with wood and grain and corn. And at first there were many letters from Kolia at the front, letters written in pencil on dirty scraps of papers, letters full of hope and enthusiasm. The armies were advancing into East Prussia, the Germans were flying before them; certainly the war would soon be over and he would return to Praskovia and never leave her again. Then the letters ceased and for a long, long time there was silence, while Praskovia's eyes grew big and hollow in her small white face, and every day a candle of yellow wax burned and flickered before the gaudily painted icon of St. Nicholas.

Then suddenly one day there came a letter again, several letters, and Praskovia knelt and cried for happiness in the shadowed, dingy church with its smell of incense and wax and humanity and dampness. Some of the hopeful buoyancy had gone from Kolia's letters now, he no longer spoke of the war being over, but Praskovia, her heart too full of the miracle that was coming to her, did not see or understand. The gray, grim winter passed; between rifts of clouds blue glimpses of sky shone out and turned the murky water to the magic colors of aquamarine and turquoise. A soft, wild wind stirred the skeleton branches of the trees, warm rain and pale sunshine flushed them to the dim rose color of bursting buds, patches of snow still lingered in the shadows, the village roads were ankle-deep in mud. And then, when the first pale green lay like the touch of magic fingers over the woods, the miracle happened and Praskovia's son was born. The bells of the little wooden church seemed to her as if they would burst their hearts with joy the day he was christened, the day when for the first time the sun really shone and the broad river and all the little puddles reflected the deep, deep blue of the sky, and the apple-blossom in the doctor's garden came out with a sudden rush.

Proud, happy letters came from Kolia at the front, letters in which he spoke only of his own joy and made no mention of the war. And then suddenly, once more there was silence, and just at first Praskovia, watching that most wonderful thing in the world, her son, did not worry. Something had happened to delay the letters, the regiment had perhaps been transferred to some more distant point in that huge line of front. It would be like the last time, and one day a letter would come again. But the days passed and lengthened and grew short and no letter came. And Praskovia held little Kolia very tightly in her arms as she gazed across the river, and kneeling before the icon of St. Nicholas the candles danced and glimmered like little golden points of fire before her tear-wet eyes. And still there was no letter, and the young green leaves withered and turned to gold, and the blue dusk slowly gathered up the hours of the ever-shortening days.

Then a little growing thrill of fear ran through the village. Terror, paralyzing and overwhelming, knocked at the low wooden doors. Women looked at each other with blanched faces. Old men muttered and shook their heads, and young boys spoke in loud, overconfident voices. For the unbelievable was happening—the Russian army was being driven back, the Germans were advancing. The news came at first as a whisper that nobody gave credence to till the first straggling groups of refugees from the villages farther south tottered along the road, with tales of fire and blood and devastation. Step by step, fighting stubbornly, magnificently, short of supplies, short of ammunition, the armies of the Little Father [Czar Nicholas II] were retreating and the gray German hordes crept forward driving the terrified people before them.

Her eyes wide and terrified, Praskovia listened. Surely such things were not possible. The Germans had come to other villages perhaps, but they would not come here—no, quite surely, St. Nicholas would protect them.

Then one day the women working in the fields heard far away on the gray horizon the thunder of the guns. The whole village came out, standing gazing across the flat green plain, listening to the sound that seemed to shake the earth they stood on. All night long it continued, and in the morning they gathered together once more, listening, watching with strained faces and sleepless eyes. Was it coming nearer? Two or three voices said it was and were contradicted by others who accused them of panic.

Then a woman, pointing down the long gray road, screamed hysterically, "What is that?" and the little crowd felt a cold air chill their spines as they saw the dark figures of horsemen and the pointing pennons of lances against the sky. "The Germans!" The words flew from mouth to mouth, seeming to paralyze action and thought. Could it be the Germans? A boy who had gone a little farther ahead and stood with his hand shading his eyes gave a laugh that was not quite natural. "No, not the Germans, some of our own men." His face a little pale above his faded green shirt, he strutted with an air of confident assurance before a group of frightened girls who clung silently together.

Rapidly the horsemen drew nearer, and the bleak wind that came with them whistled along the road and set the long grasses shivering as at the approach of something sinister and terrible. Roughly they drove their tired, shaggy horses into the group of brightly clad women. "The Germans are coming," they cried. "Our army is in full retreat. You must leave this village at once. We are burning everything as we go, so that the swine shall find nothing but ruins when they come."

The words with all their portent of ruin and disaster were received in stricken silence, then somewhere a woman began to cry silently, apathetically, resignedly, and an old man railed at Fate in a thin, high-pitched, shaking voice.

And thereafter a hurried, panic-stricken gathering together of household goods, horses or cows harnessed to the low wooden carts, children clasping cats or chickens in their arms bundled in, useless things that could not possibly be wanted loaded up with care while the very necessaries of life were left behind. Babies crying, women scolding, old men hobbling wistfully about and getting in everybody's way, and always on the gray horizon the thunder of guns and the shrieking wind that seemed to bring with it all kinds of nightmare terrors.

≈

The short gray autumn day sank into darkness; before them there was only the uneven, stony road, behind them a red glare in the sky at which they dared not look! And day by day along that road of terror and despair the crowd grew denser; plodding along with no hope in the future, suffering, enduring, dying. Deserted, overturned carts, scattered household property, dead or dying horses, a lost dog or cat with barely enough strength to crawl, an old woman sitting by the roadside mumbling inarticulate words, a hurriedly made grave, or perhaps no grave at all but just a dead body lying with sightless eyes turned up to the gray monotony of sky. These things increased also as day by day hunger and exhaustion and disease stalked among that pitiful throng. Was it real or only a dream, so hideous as to seem impossible! With shoes long since worn through to shreds, Praskovia limped along, her numbed arms carrying little Kolia—a burden that grew every day a little lighter. Big Kolia's mother had died of fever and exhaustion very soon, and at last they told Praskovia that little Kolia was dead too, that she need not carry him any farther. But she could not believe them. "He is only asleep," she whispered in her hoarse, strained voice and held him closer to her breast. "Do not wake him."

They managed finally to get the poor little body away from her, and somebody got her a place in one of the carts, where she lay babbling in fevered delirium till they reached the railway and were all packed into dark, evil-smelling cattle-trucks [cars]. But she, whose prayer was that she should die, retained against her will her hold on life, came back from her fevered unconsciousness to the knowledge of a bare, bleak shed filled with that ever-present crowd of men, women, and children. The end of the journey was reached and Praskovia's eyes brightened when they told her that they were in Petrograd, for dimly she held to a far-off hope that here in the capital she would perhaps get news of big Kolia, or if not any definite news, at least some breath or glimmer that would tell her what his fate had been.

Very vague, very dim, very unreal were these hopes, built more on fairy-tales than on actual possibilities, visions of an All-seeing Little Father who would send her word where Kolia was. Dreams of some big gray-haired general who would dispatch a mounted rider to bring him back from that terrible, far-distant line of battle. Dreams and visions all broken into rainbow fragments against the inflexible wall of facts, the callous iron circle of official listlessness and negligence. And yet Praskovia's child-like faith in humankind was not to be quite utterly shattered. One of the many officials she went to see happened to be a colonel of infantry gifted with imagination. True, he could give her no answer to her so oft-repeated question! Her husband had been with the army in Galicia? She had not heard from him for seven months! The colonel shook his head. He would make what inquiries he could, but he knew that the general of that division had been killed in the retreat, and among so many million men

[Historians estimate that some 20,000,000 Russians died during this period]. . . . He raised his shoulders, and then, glancing at the white face and haunted eyes, he asked one or two questions, gathered the whole pitiful story and remained silent for a moment, frowning at the pile of papers on his desk. At last, after what seemed to Praskovia an endless pause, he scribbled a few words on a card and handed it to her. "That's where I live," he told her. "I have heard my wife say she was in need of a girl to help in the house. Come there tomorrow morning."

So Praskovia found shelter and a home. Placid, gentle-faced Madame Ivanoff took her to her motherly heart, the work was light, and the hollows of Praskovia's cheeks filled out, and her step lost its dragging listlessness. But nothing would ease the ache of loneliness in her heart, nothing could replace the tiny clutching fingers at her breast, or the love she had read in big Kolia's eyes—Kolia who perhaps lay out yonder on that unknown line of battle, done to death by a German shell.

≈

But Kolia was not dead! Fighting grimly, hopelessly, without arms or ammunition [this military unpreparedness for the conflict helped bring about the fall of the Romanov dynasty], he had been wounded and taken prisoner by the Germans. For an endless time he had lain between life and death in a filthy prison-camp, alternately raving in a delirium or apathetic in a state of coma, till at last he won through and emerged a ghost with yellow, wasted cheeks and hollow eyes.

Days, weeks, and months dragged themselves away in an unending sameness, during which he lost hope and courage and the count of time. There were French and British in the same camp who got letters and parcels to lighten the deadly monotony. But for Kolia nothing came, and the world outside the barbed wire seemed utterly empty, while the world inside was just an endless passing of weary, hopeless hours. He wrote many letters and was told that perhaps they would be sent, but whether they were or whether they ever reached their destination he did not know, and certainly no answer ever came.

How long he was in that prison-camp Kolia never quite knew, but after a little more than a year his chance came and, spurred by a sudden desperation, he took it, and he and a big red-bearded Cossack got away. For two days and a half they lay hidden in a hole in the ground, listening with pounding hearts to the search that swept to and fro above them, with only one dry biscuit between them. Then at last, with parched tongues and cracked lips, they crept out at night and started on their tramp toward the vague direction of the French lines. That first drink at a little muddy pool, would Kolia ever forget it? That first dawn in the forest with the sleepy twitter of waking birds calling to each other from tree to tree, who could explain the rapture of it?

Living like hunted animals, eating grass and roots, they plodded on, escaping by purest chance the troops of soldiers who pervaded everything. And then, when that longed-for frontier line lay only ten miles away, the Cossack's strength gave out. For days he had stumbled on, racked by a burning fever to which he had refused to give in. Only to reach the frontier! he whispered hoarsely. Then they would send him back to Russia quickly—oh, yes, very quickly—and once there he could die in peace. But he must get back to Russia—he must not die in the enemy's land. For the last day Kolia almost carried him, listening always to those broken, mumbling words, with a heart too full of dull, apathetic pain to find any answer or comfort. And then quite suddenly and quietly the hoarse voice broke off into silence, the tall figure worn to a pitiful ghost of rag and bone crumpled up, and Kolia, looking down into the white face that was so suddenly at peace, knelt beside him to whisper a broken, disjointed prayer, and then, with shaking, trembling limbs, crept on.

And Kolia got through—by what miracle of luck it is hard to say—walking straight with blind, unseeing eyes into a patrol of French soldiers, who took him at first for a wandering ghost. And finally, after much delay, he was shipped to England among some other poor scarecrows like himself, and there they were fed and clothed and cared for and at last sent off on their homeward journey across Sweden and Norway, strange, unknown countries they had never heard of. A long, weary, endless journey, till at last on a bleak November day they crossed the frontier up at that desolate northern point of Finland with its huge snow-covered plains and its broad, frozen river with the straggling wooden villages on either side.

Russia—his own mother country—Praskovia and the son he had never seen! Kolia drew a big, deep breath, the blue eyes that had gone so far back into his head alight with an incredulous happiness. Surely they would allow him to go back to his village just for a very little while. And then he would fight once more for the Little Father. He would be glad to fight again, his hatred of the Germans increased tenfold since the long torture of the prison-camp.

But when he came to Petrograd with its golden domes and spires and red and yellow palaces, he was told that his village had been for over a year in German hands, and nobody could tell him any news of his wife and child. Most likely they had escaped, but where they were who could tell? There had been so many refugees and Russia was so big.

The light went out of Kolia's sky, utter hopelessness descended on his spirit, and with it a dull, sullen anger, a smouldering resentment that slowly grew and grew.

For weeks they kept him waiting with hundreds of his other comrades, till somebody had time to think which front they should be sent to. Several times Kolia went to the wooden barracks near the Warsaw station where many of the refugees still lived, but nobody could tell him anything of Praskovia. There had been so many hundred refugees and so many had died on the way, and many had gone to other towns and many had been here and left. Praskovia Ivanoff and a baby—God help us, but how was one to remember a name? From the village of Krassnitz? There were no other refugees from that village here. There had been some but they had gone. Where to? God knows! They had found other work perhaps or they had died. Praskovia Ivanoff—somebody dimly remembered the name, but she had had no child with her, that was certain, and she had gone away long ago.

At last, when the drifting ice on the river had frozen into a solid mass, Kolia was sent to the front, and, that smouldering resentment still hot within him, he went, dull, apathetic, utterly indifferent.

The winter dragged itself away till the revolution swept everything before it. But even that could not stir Kolia from his listlessness. What was the good of liberty to him now? They told him that the Emperor had abdicated and he frowned in perplexed wonder. Why, that would mean there would be no Little Father—and what was the meaning of the word *republic*?

And then a dirty-looking man with greasy black hair and narrow, shifting eyes came and spoke to the regiment, standing on a wooden bench and pouring forth a torrent of suave speech. And at first Kolia did not understand or even listen very much, but little by little the smooth words began to sink in and woke that dull, sullen anger of his to life. Why should they go on fighting now? The Germans were ready and willing to make peace. It was only England and France who for their own vainglorious ends wished to prolong the horror of the war. Russia was no longer bound to them. It was the Emperor's government who had made the Alliance, and the Emperor's government did not exist. Russia was free now, and to every one of her citizens would be given bread in plenty and land and peace. Germany would withdraw her armies and give back the conquered territory—give back the conquered territory! That sentence broke through the fog in Kolia's brain. That meant his village also—the woods and the green fields and the river—and perhaps—perhaps, after all, Praskovia was still there—and his old mother.

The man with the oily black hair and the narrow eyes left them; but another one came, apparently from nowhere, a huge, burly-looking fellow this, with a bristling black beard and fierce, bloodshot eyes. In a hoarse, raucous voice he spoke to the soldiers, and his words were all fire and sedition. They had been tortured and downtrodden long enough, but the day of liberation was at hand, the day when the aggressors would pay in blood, and again more blood. The war had been waged by the capitalists for their own ends. The soldiers who had fought and suffered were to get nothing from it; let the soldiers, there-fore, end it and take for themselves their reward. A day of glory was to dawn for Russia; first among all the nations, she would teach the world the meaning of democracy.

This man in time also left them, but others took his place, and always there were the same glowing promises, the same picture of peace and plenty painted on a screen of fire. And the soldiers listened and believed and followed the gleaming will-o'-the-wisp that was to lead them into the swamp of anarchy and destruction—and Kolia, sullen, embittered, indifferent, followed after them.

≈

The blue river hurried on swiftly, silently, to the sea; above the Winter Palace a torn rag of crimson fluttered against the pale, pure sky. Now and then a hot, dry wind blew a cloud of evil-smelling dust along the deserted quays. Hardly a sound broke the utter silence. There were no boats on the river, there were no carriages in the streets, the windows of the palace stared out with blind eyes upon a world of desolation, here and there a torn blind flapped forlornly, a broken pane of glass showed a chasm of darkness.

Slowly Kolia walked down the quay, his shoulders bent, his feet dragging wearily in their torn boots on the hot, dirty pavement. At rare intervals people passed him, men or women who looked at him furtively, anxiously, and went on their way, haunted eyes always watching the shadows of the great doorways. At one corner the dead body of a horse lay on the pavement, and Kolia turned away because he could not bear to see the human scavengers who surrounded it.

Where was he going? He did not know or care, his brain was just a confused, chaotic emptiness in which only one thought burned like a flame of red-hot pain. They had killed the Emperor, they had murdered him cruelly with his wife and children. Kolia had deadened pity and compassion long ago; drunk with wine and the bitterness of his own wrongs, he had killed and seen kill, and only hardened himself to a fiercer anger. But now suddenly his eyes were opened, and the light that faced them was a glare of intolerable anguish that blinded him with vain regret and shame.

On he stumbled, past the red, battered Winter Palace, past the great, silent building of the Admiralty, past the statue of

Peter the Great, till suddenly his steps were brought up short at the end of the quay, and there was only before him a little white church standing amongst green trees; and Kolia, obeying some dumb instinct that craved for shelter and relief from the hot glare of the desolate, dirty streets, went in.

The door yielded to his touch, silence and darkness met him, the golden-painted icons gleamed dimly out of the shadows, on the walls the engraved names of the sailors who had died during the Japanese War were hidden under a coating of dust; no glimmer of light burned anywhere in the deserted emptiness of this church built to the memory of men who had given their lives for the empire that had crumbled away.

Before the golden icon of St. Nicholas Kolia paused and silently knelt down. Was not St. Nicholas his patron saint, even as he was the patron saint of the murdered Emperor? In the gilt stand in front of the silent image there were the burned-out rests of one or two candles, and vaguely Kolia wondered who had put them there and wished he had a candle, too. For a long time he knelt there and could find no prayer in the aching void of his mind. What was there he could pray for in a world that was so dark and tortured? And then unconsciously almost he began to pray for the impossible to happen, and, knowing well that it was impossible, found yet a certain comfort in it. "Holy St. Nicholas," he whispered, "have mercy on me–forgive me– have mercy upon me and bring Praskovia back to me——" And so over and over again till the mere fact that he was praying began to ease his tortured mind.

The door of the church had opened very softly, somebody came in and crept forward, but Kolia did not move; only, listening to the faint sounds, he thought that whoever it was must be very tired, for they moved so slowly. Somebody paused behind him, there was a little fumbling, rustling sound, then a match scraped, a faint light wavered like a golden shadow in the grayness, a trembling hand placed a little yellow candle before the image of St. Nicholas.

Kolia watched it and wondered. He had thought that in this dead city of despair nobody prayed any more. Who was it who had still enough courage and hope left? But the woman who knelt beside him in the shadows had a heavy gray shawl covering her bent head, and the thick folds hid her face from his tired, curious eyes.

So for a few silent minutes the man and the woman knelt beside each other in the deserted church, while the solitary candle wavered and flickered this way and that, a poor, lonely little prayer in the emptiness of eternity.

Down and down it burned, the cheap inferior wax dripping on the floor, and at last with a feeble sputter and hiss went out, leaving behind it a wreath of blue, acrid-smelling smoke.

With a sigh that was utterly weary the woman rose and, without knowing why he did it, Kolia rose, too, and followed her. Her hand on the heavy door, she felt him close behind her and turned, fear lending her a desperate courage. "What is it you want?" she whispered, and remained suddenly silent, staring up at him with wide, dark eyes. "It—" she began, and then her voice broke. "Kolia—it can't be you—is it *you*?"

He was on his knees before her now, his trembling arms flung round her, his tear-wet, ravaged face pressed into the folds of her skirt, and, incapable of speech, she laid her hands on his rough, tumbled hair.

Words, explanations, questions, answers—all these were to come later: the story of his imprisonment and escape, of her having to leave the village, of the refuge she had found, her life with her employers on their estate, the murder of the kind old colonel by pillaging soldiers, her flight with his widow to humble lodgings in the city.

For all these there would be time later. For the present they only knew that they had found each other, that the miracle they had prayed for had come to pass. And perhaps in the shadow St. Nicholas smiled with an infinity of compassion and understanding."[10]

CONCLUSION

The Apostle of Anonymous Giving

Why do we still remember Nicholas after seventeen hundred years? Not because he was a martyr, not because he was a miracle worker, not because he was a great achiever, not because he was eloquent. Instead, we remember him because early in life he immersed himself in the four Gospels and internalized the way of life Christ postulated in Matthew, Mark, Luke, and John.

At the heart of the Gospels is servanthood. Over and over Christ hammered home, both in abstractions and stories, the great truth that just as He, our Master, came to serve rather than be served, just so, we ought to follow that divine example.

Against no sin did Christ thunder more than the sin of pride. And pride is the central reason why it is so incredibly difficult for human beings to give anonymously. We all want our reward in the here and now. We all want a plaque on the wall testifying to our generosity. We want all those we seek to impress (which is just about everyone) to know just how generous we are. We give mainly to those who can afford to give gifts back, preferably of as great or greater value than the gifts we bestowed on them.

This trait evidences itself mighty early in life: everything we do—even if it is nothing more than losing a tooth, stubbing a toe, banging into a table, jumping off a diving board—*has* to have an audience: "Look, Mom!" "Look, Dad!" "Look!" "Look!" "Look!" Nothing means anything to us unless others notice: sort of like hitting a hole in one when we're alone—it's hollow because we know no one will believe our unsubstantiated story.

Consequently, as we grow older, we continually bask—perhaps even wallow—in our acknowledged good deeds. Speaking just for myself, I can't think of any challenge life has brought me more difficult to deal with than the issue of credit. No matter how many times I determine to follow Christ's injunction to only give anonymously, I'm always looking around, hoping someone has noticed. Only God has the power to grant such self-lessness to those of us who earnestly seek it and ignominiously fail, time after time, to follow through without surreptitiously looking back to see if some blessed public relations person just happened to see and chronicle it.

From all indications, St. Nicholas is one of the very few human beings on record who has ever been able to sustain such sublimation of self for a lifetime. We are told that the incidents having to do with the story of the three dowerless daughters represented but one of many such selfless acts in his life. Collectively, these simple but almost impossible to perform acts added up to immortality. For, as they say, *to live on in the hearts of others—is not to die.*

Down through history, there have been other voices raised in support of such values:

ST. FRANCIS OF ASSISI (1181–1226), WHO MEMORABLY PRAYED,

Lord,
Make me an instrument of Your peace.
Where there is hatred, let me sow love;
Where there is injury, pardon;
Where there is doubt, faith;
Where there is despair, hope;
Where there is darkness, light; and
Where there is sadness, joy.
O' divine Master,
Grant that I may not so much
Seek to be consoled as to console;
To be understood as to understand;
To be loved as to love;
For it is in giving that we receive;
It is in pardoning that we are pardoned; and
It is in dying that we are born to eternal life.

And in modern times, there is Charles Dickens (1812–1870), who, in his immortal *Christmas Carol* (1843), pointed out that life can be lived fully only by the act of selfless giving to others.

In the late nineteenth century, Henry Van Dyke (1852–1933) wrote *The Other Wise Man* (1892), depicting a fourth member of the Magi, Artaban, who, like St. Nicholas, was convicted that selfless giving to, and ministering to, the Lord's sheep was the highest calling. Eighteen years later, Van Dyke tackled the central issue of St. Nicholas's life: Christ's repeated injunctions to give only in secret, for only thus can your treasure be stored in heaven. The book *The Mansion* (1910) tells the story of a man who is determined to secure simultaneous credit on earth and heaven for his good works. (These two small masterpieces represent the greatest one-two punch in all Christmas literature.)

Nineteen years later Lloyd C. Douglas (1877–1951) addressed the same subject in *Magnificent Obsession* (1929). In the novel Douglas depicts the life of a doctor who refuses to accept public credit for acts done in secret, because he's already been recompensed inwardly by God. To belatedly be given credit in public would be tantamount to canceling out the spiritual blessing. Ten years later Douglas would revisit the issue in *Dr. Hudson's Secret Journal* (1939). Both Douglas and Van Dyke maintain it is impossible to outgive God.

≈

Now, let's fast-forward seventy years to the Veggie Tales' DVD *Saint Nicholas: A Story of Joyful Giving* (Big Idea, 2009), and the companion book, Matthew West's *Give This Christmas Away* (Tyndale House, 2009), both inspired by Franklin Graham's Operation Christmas Child (OCC), dedicated to showing the world how to change your life by abandoning passive receiving in favor of active giving. All three preach St. Nicholas's message of anonymous giving.

West's *Give This Christmas Away* is a small but powerful must-read, mainly because he moves beyond stereotypical giving by suggesting 101 ways in which we may imitate St. Nicholas by selfless giving in our own lives. Practical down-home suggestions such as (1) join OCC and fill up shoeboxes with things such as toys, toothbrushes, and school supplies, and send them to destitute children around the world; (2) in the middle of the night during blizzards, secretly shovel driveways of neighbors who are elderly or incapacitated; (3) visit seniors who are alone or in assisted-living facilities at Christmas; (4) volunteer at a homeless shelter *after* Christmas; (5) kids, write out "work" coupons to give to your parents; (6) bake an extra dozen cookies, and give the entire dozen away; (7) surprise people by secretly paying their restaurant tabs; (8) every day in December, tell someone in your life that you love him or her; (9) park in the back instead of always grabbing the closest parking space; (10) offer to babysit free for a couple with young children so they may enjoy a much-needed night out. And West suggests ninety-one more ways to change your part of the world.

≈

For all these reasons and more, we remember and seek to emulate the life and example of St. Nicholas of Myra. St. Nicholas, who even after seventeen hundred years, shows no signs of going away.

APPENDIX

Resources

A NEW KIND OF CHRISTMAS SEASON

Many families today are seeking more in their annual celebrations of Christmas than conspicuous consumption and reminders of X-number of shopping days until Christmas. The heretofore missing dimension of Nicholastide, bookended by Christmastide, is a three-part celebration.

First: Nicholastide will begin on November 16 and end on December 6, St. Nicholas day. The Season of the Advent, normally the twenty-four days concluding with December 25, is second. Third is Christmastide, also called "The Twelve Days of Christmas," which begins on December 26 and concludes January 6 with Epiphany. Much more specific ideas for implementing such a season can be found in our companion book: Joe Wheeler and Jim Rosenthal's *St. Nicholas: A Closer Look at Christmas* (Thomas Nelson, 2005).

If such a tripartite Christmas season is to succeed, it must be seamless, from the same metaphorical bolt of cloth. It will be almost like entering another country, dimension, or time warp, every November 16. Parents must be united in their determination to remain solidly in control of every aspect of it, otherwise the entire construct will collapse like the proverbial house of cards. An overall atmosphere of serenity is the ideal. Come each evening, a fire should be lit in the fireplace, kerosene lamps should be lit, or low-light lamps turned on. Electronic media of *all kinds*, including the telephone, should generally be off. Only emergencies or absolute necessities should be permitted to take any family member, young or old, away from the family hearth. Appropriate music, used judiciously, will enhance the season, as will evening board games, a great way to bond. Surprisingly, it has been discovered that children brag to their friends about such electronically controlled serenity—it is something unique in their too-often noise-filled lives. And children do not spell love L-O-V-E, but rather T-I-M-E; consequently, when parents devote their time to them, what's not to like about that?

STORYTIME

Once upon a time—and not that long ago at that—the fireplace, kitchen stove, or home library was the center of family life. Story time was held sacred, occurring each night of the children's growing-up years. Parents then understood a great truth that appears to be all but forgotten today: every day, every hour, every moment, of their growing-up years, children are *becoming*. Indeed, it is no hyperbole to say they are the sum total of what they are exposed to. We become our favorite stories. The stories your children love most will inevitably become woven into their characters. Sadly, if we permit the media to be the storyteller to our children, we are not feeding them with values worth living by. Such values come from a daily parent-directed story hour, centered around a continually growing family library of books worth reading and rereading, and stories they never tire of hearing. To assume a media center dominated by a wide-screen television set can possibly be a valid substitute for the family story hour would be a tragic misperception. And the family discussions resulting from such reading have a staggering impact on the character of each growing child.

NICHOLASTIDE

Suggestions:

- Adopt the old Irish tradition of lighting a candle in the window on the first night of Nicholastide (read Margaret Sangster's "Like a Candle in the Window"). [*See the suggested story resources at the end of this section.] Continue to light this candle every evening during our fifty-two days of Christmas.
- Read a story each evening from the many St. Nicholas stories in this book (especially "The Three Dowerless Daughters") and also from the twenty-three listed Stories of Anonymous Giving.
- Thanksgiving (in mid-Nicholastide) deserves special emphasis. We have listed five Thanksgiving stories to draw from.

- Consider adopting "The Last Straw" tradition in your own family. See Paula McDonald Palangi's story by that title (under "Suggested Story Resources," p. 162).
- Consider making up a Nicholastide calendar similar to the Advent one.
- Many churches and communities schedule St. Nicholas cookie exchanges no later than December 3 or 4, so all families may enjoy a variety of cookie types at home.
- Consider adopting the English tradition of each family member, young or old, bringing a *new* toy to a special church service; then distribute them to needy children.
- Encourage each family member to adopt the concept of the Nicholas-related baker's dozen: give more than is required, much as Christ advocated volunteering for a second mile when required to do only one.
- Since the stocking ritual dates back to St. Nicholas, celebrate it on St. Nicholas Eve on December 5, encouraging each family member to anonymously contribute handmade gifts. Have a special St. Nicholas Eve dinner and program as well.

ADVENT

- Begin Advent either twenty-four days before December 25 or on Thanksgiving Night. On that night, set up the crèche or nativity scene.
- On each night, read a story from the two lists: 40 Stories

of Sacrificial Giving and 26 Stories for Advent or Christmastide.

- Purchase an Advent wreath, five Advent candles (one white, one rose, and three purple), an Advent calendar, and Christmas carol songbooks.

- Beginning on the second evening of Advent, parents with small children set in motion a long journey from the remotest rooms of the house, each of the three Magi from a different room: Caspar from the most remote room, Melchior in a second, and Balthasar in a third (all originating from various parts of ancient Persia). The family will carefully choreograph each one's journey (using maps), discussing geography, climates, dangers, cities, etc., each day, being careful to plan ahead so each of the Magi arrives to meet the others in Bethlehem on Epiphany. Read Henry VanDyke's *The Other Wise Man*.

- Act out St. Luke's gospel. Children love to dramatize events and stories.

- Consider acting out Mexico's greatest Christmas tradition, *Las Posadas*, beginning the eve of December 16. Read my Christmas story, "Posada," for details.

- Also consider acting out that beloved Polish contribution to Christmas "The Star Boys" or the *Szopka*. Read Kelly's "The Christmas Nightingale" and "In Clean Hay." (See page 162.)

- On Christmas Eve, read Bill Vaughan's "Tell Me a Story

of Christmas" (See page 164.) just before reading Luke's nativity story.

- Consider playing the Trading Game each Christmas. See my "Hans and the Trading Game" story. (See page 163.)

CHRISTMASTIDE

- Continue reading (or dramatizing) a story every evening.
- Consider giving a special (handmade if possible) gift to your beloved each of the Twelve Days of Christmas. Sing and get everyone to act out the gift-giving in that carol.
- On St. Stephen's Day (the first day of Christmastide), encourage everyone—in memory of the first Christmas martyr—to pray for those they dislike. Also have each family member place one of their choicest presents in what's called "St. Stephen's Box," to be given to unfortunate families.
- On *Childermas* (the third day of Christmas), share with your children the story of Herod's slaughter of all the boy babies in Bethlehem.
- On New Year's Eve, have each person discuss what went well in the old year, and what didn't, and come up with resolutions likely to be kept. Choose from the 10 New Year's stories.
- On Epiphany, have the Magi arrive at the stable.
- Consider scheduling Twelfth Night activities, such as

electing a Bean King or Bean Queen. Or if children are involved, have those who bite down on a bean in their piece of cake assume the role of one of the Magi for the evening.

• On Epiphany Night, read that greatest of all Epiphany Christmas stories, Turnbull's "Merry Little Christmas." (See page 165.) When the last line is read, blow out the candle in the window for the last time.

But 312 days later, St. Nicholas will bring the Christmas season back again.

~

SUGGESTED STORY RESOURCES

Many Christmas stories with an emphasis on spiritual values are found in my Christmas in My Heart series.

Note: "C" stands for *Christmas in My Heart*. C-1 would mean *Christmas in My Heart 1*.

NICHOLASTIDE STORIES, EMPHASIZING SELFLESS ANONYMOUS GIVING LIST #1

C-1 "The Promise of the Doll"—Ruth Ikerman; C-2 "The Last Straw"—Paula McDonald Palangi; C-3 "Rebecca's Only Way"—Annie Hamilton Donnell; "A Gift from the Heart"—Norman Vincent Peale; C-4 "Christmas Day in the Morning"—Pearl Buck; C-7 "The Red Envelope"—Nancy Rue; C-8 "Why the Chimes Rang"—Raymond McDonald

Alden; "Feels Good in My Heart"—Wendy Miller; C-9 "Bulger's Friends"—O. Henry; C-10 "No Man Need Walk Alone"—Seth Parker; C-11 "The Ragged Red Coat"—Karen A. Williams; C-12 "Our Part in the Circle"—Joyce Reagin; C-13 "Colin's Christmas Candle"—Barbara Raftery; "The Thin Little Lonely One"— Annie Hamilton Donnell; C-14 "The Night My Father Came Home"—Author Unknown; C-15 "Miracle at Midnight"— Camilla R. Bittle; "Carla's Gift"—Torey Hayden; C-16 "Flocks by Night"—Bruce Douglas; "The Mansion"—Henry Van Dyke; C-17 "President for One Hour"—Fred P. Fox; "In Clean Hay"— Eric P. Kelly; C-18 "Oren's Christmas Present"—Idona Hill; "An Exchange of Gifts"—Diane Rayner.* Besides the life stories of St. Nicholas in this book, also share the story "The Three Dowerless Daughters" (pp. 19-21) with your children.

Thanksgiving Stories

Great Stories Remembered I, "The Widened Hearth"—Fannie H. Kilbourne; "The Thankful Book"—Helen Peck. *Great Stories Remembered II*, "Home for Thanksgiving"—L. D. Stearns.

Great Stories Remembered III, "Harvest Home Harmony"— Margaret E. Sangster.

Smoky, the Ugliest Cat in the World and Other Great Cat Stories, "Thankful Cats"—Abbie Farwell Brown [Pacific Press Publishing].

Advent and Christmastide Stories of Sacrificial Giving

C-1 "A Certain Small Shepherd"—Rebecca Caudill;

"A String of Blue Beads"—Fulton Oursler; "The Why of Christmas"—Don Dedera; "Bethany's Christmas Carol"—Mabel McKee; C-2 "The Gift of the Magi"—O. Henry; "Christmas Magic"—Christine Whiting Parmenter; "A Small Gift of Love"—Mary Ellen Holmes; C-3 "Yet Not One of Them Shall Fall"—Hartley Dailey; "The Story of the Other Wise Man"—Henry Van Dyke; C-4 "Charlie's Blanket"—Wendy Miller; "Unlucky Jim"—Arthur Maxwell; C-5 "A Christmas Miracle"—Kathleen Ruckman; "Under the Banana Leaf Christmas Tree"—Carolyn Rathbun; "Hans and the Trading Game"—Joe Wheeler; C-6 "Their Best Christmas"—Hartley Dailey; "How Far Is It to Bethlehem?"—Elizabeth Orton Jones; C-7 "Kashara's Gift"—Lissa Halls Johnson; "Anniversary"—Margaret Sangster Jr.; C-9 "His Guiding Star"—Mary Agnes Jackman; C-10 "Terry"—Frank McMillan; C-11 "Lipstick Like Lindsay's"—Gerald Toner; C-12 "Joyful *and* Triumphant,"—John McCain; C-13 "Kitten of Bethlehem"—Ruth Ikerman; "Our POW Christmas"—Christine Helsby; "The Rescue of Mr. Christmas"—Josephine Cunnington Edwards; "The Doll with No Face"—Kathleen Ruckman; C-14 "A Boy Named John"—Author Unknown; C-15 "Forty Dollars to Spend"—Shirley Seifert; "Please, Sir, I Want to Buy a Miracle"—Albert Stauderman; "The Forgotten Santa"—Author Unknown; C-16 "Christmas in the Street of Memories"—Elizabeth Rhodes Jackson; "The Layaway Doll"—Marlene Chase; "A Cake of Pink Soap"—Author Unknown; "A Very Special Present"—Ingrid Tomey; "Bless the Child"—Isobel Stewart; C-17 "The Cherry-Colored

Purse"—Alice Josephine Johnson; C-18 "The Christmas
Rose"—Marlene Chase; "Plum Pudding for Posterity"—
Mabel McKee; "And Glory Shone All Around"—Christine
Whiting Parmenter; C-19 "A Bride Doll Just for Looking
At"—Connie Lounsbury; "A Christmas Conscience"—J. L.
Harbour; "The Layette"—Marlene Chase.

Nativity Stories For Advent And Christmastide

C-1 "A Certain Small Shepherd"—Rebecca Caudill; "Guest
in the House"—Ruth Emery Amanrude; C-2 "The Tallest
Angel"—Author Unknown; "Tell Me a Story of Christmas"—
Bill Vaughan; C-3 "Star Across the Tracks"—Bess Streeter
Aldrich; C-4 "Trouble at the Inn"—Dina Donahue; "Pink
Angel"—Author Unknown; C-5 "Christmas Angel"—Ethelyn
M. Parkinson; "Something Quite Forgotten"—Grace Livingston
Hill; C-7 "The First Creche"—Arthur Gordon; C-8 "A Girl Like
Me"—Nancy Rue; C-9 "Christmas Is for Kids"—Nancy Rue;
C-10 "The Best Christmas Pageant Ever"—Barbara Robinson;
C-12 "The Story of the Field of Angels"—Florence Morse
Kingsley; C-13 "The Night the Stars Sang"—Dorothy Canfield
Fisher; "Kitten of Bethlehem"—Ruth Ikerman; "Surprise
Christmas"—Mary Geisler Phillips; C-15 "Eric's Gift"—Debbie
Smoot; "The Christmas Pageant"—Michael Lindvall; C-16
"When the Wise Man Appeared"—William Ashley Anderson;
"Christmas in a Pickle Jar"—Emily Buck; "Bless the Child"—
Isobel Stewart; C-17 "The Magic of the Season"—Isobel Stewart;
"Through the Mike"—Ruth Herrick Myers; "The Rugged

Road"—Margaret Sangster; C-19 "The Layette"—Marlene Chase; "The Philosopher's Awakening"—Mabel Lee Cooper.

NEW YEAR'S, NEW BEGINNINGS (EPIPHANY) STORIES

Great Stories Remembered I, "Last Day on Earth"—Frances Ancker and Cynthia Hope; "Boy on the Running Board"—Annie Hamilton Donnell; "Monty Price's Nightingale"—Zane Grey; *Great Stories Remembered II*, "In a Chinese Garden"—Frederic Loomis; "Revolutions"—Ida Alexander; *Great Stories Remembered III*, "Family Ties"—P. J. Platz; "The Leaf That Mother Turned"—Annie Hamilton Donnell; "The Unmousing of Jean"—Edna Geister; *Heart to Heart Stories for Mothers*, "When Queens Ride By"—Agnes Sligh Turnbull; C-5 "Merry Little Christmas"—Agnes Sligh Turnbull.

Publishers for all these stories and books: *Christmas in My Heart 1–16*, Review and Herald Publishing, Hagerstown, MD, and Pacific Press Publishing, Nampa, ID, for *Christmas in My Heart 17–19*. Other sources referred to are *Great Stories Remembered I, II, III, Heart to Heart Stories for Mothers*, published by Focus on the Family/Tyndale House. All these books are also available direct from Joe Wheeler (Sage and Holly Distributors, P.O. Box 1246, Conifer, CO 80433).

NOTES

Introduction: Did St. Nicholas Really Live?

1. Seal, *Nicholas*, 15.
2. Durant, *The Age of Faith*, 62.
3. *Encyclopedia Britannica*, vol. 16, 416.

Chapter 1: The Azure Coast

1. Miller and Lane, *Harper's Bible Dictionary*, 529–34; Barnes, *The Historical Atlas of the Bible*, 304–5.
2. "50 Places of a Lifetime," *National Geographic Traveler*, October 2009.
3. Crichton, *Who Is Santa Claus*, 17.
4. Ibid., 17–18; Cann, *Saint Nicholas*, 25–32.
5. Cann, *Saint Nicholas, Bishop of Myra*, 33–34.
6. Ibid., 38–39.

Chapter 2: The Boy Bishop

1. Cann, *Saint Nicholas*, 45–47.

Chapter 3: Kept Alive by Stories

1. Cann, *Saint Nicholas*, 192–93.
2. Ibid., 195–96.

Chapter 4: Nicholas and Constantine

1. Durant, *The Age of Faith*, 3–6.
2. Seal, *The Epic Journey from Saint to Santa Claus*, 64–65.
3. Ibid.

4. Ebon, *Saint Nicholas, Life and Legend*, 34–35.
5. Cann, *Saint Nicholas*, 111–15.
6. Adapted from Markou, *Concerning the Relics of St. Nicholas*, 20–21.
7. Sources for this chapter: Durant, *Caesar and Christ*, 639–68; Durant, *The Age of Faith*, 3–10; *Encyclopedia Britannica*, vol. 19, 505; *Encyclopedia Britannica*, vol. 23, 793; Jones, *St. Nicholas of Bari*, 9, 18, 19, 27, 32–33, 35, 38, 42, 63, 70, 82, 94, 298–99; Voragine, *Golden Legend*, n.p.

CHAPTER 5: BYZANTINE AUTUMN

1. Durant, *The Age of Faith*, 103–17, 129–31, 426.
2. Hole, 1.
3. Jones, *St. Nicholas of Bari*, 74–75.
4. Ebon, *Saint Nicholas*, 50–52.

CHAPTER 6: ST. NICHOLAS MOVES WEST

1. Creasy, *The Fifteen Decisive Battles of the World*, 93–108.
2. Jones, *St. Nicholas of Bari*, 227; Robinson, 100–10.
3. Cioffari, *Saint Nicholas: His Life, the Translation of His Relics and His Basilica in Bari*, 53–68.
4. Jones, *St. Nicholas of Bari*, 194.
5. Ibid.
6. Cioffari, *Saint Nicholas*, 57–58; Jones, *St. Nicholas of Bari*, 216.

CHAPTER 7: ST. NICHOLAS AT FLOODTIDE

1. Jones, *St. Nicholas of Bari*, 370; Ebon, *Saint Nicholas*, 53, 60.
2. LeMoy, *L'Anjou*
3. Jones, *St. Nicholas of Bari*, 99–107, 148, 160.
4. Ibid., 238–39.
5. Ibid., 240–45.
6. Ibid., 116–18.
7. Howard Pyle, *Harper's Young People*, vol. vii, 415–17.
8. Jones, *St. Nicholas of Bari*, 144.
9. Pyle, *Harper's Young People*, vol. vii, 205.
10. Ancelet-Hustache, *Saint Nicholas*, 82.

CHAPTER 8: FIGHTING FOR SURVIVAL

1. Jones, *St. Nicholas of Bari*, 285–86.

CHAPTER 9: ST. NICHOLAS IN THE NEW WORLD

1. Bennett, *The True Saint Nicholas*, 96–97.
2. Ebon, *Saint Nicholas*, 94.
3. Jones, *St. Nicholas of Bari*, 344–45.
4. Armstrong, "A Christmas Visit," 11.
5. Copied from Clement Clark Moore's *The Night Before Christmas* (Philadelphia: Porter & Coates, 1883).
6. Mark Arnest, 8.
7. Nissenbaum, *The Battle for Christmas*, 71–86.
8. *New York Sun* September 21, 1897.
9. Ebon, *Saint Nicholas*, 106–7.
10. Moffatt, *Norman Rockwell*, n.p.

CHAPTER 10: ST. NICHOLAS TODAY

1. *Christmas in the Netherlands*, 13.
2. Ibid., 8.
3. Ibid., 14.
4. Ibid., 1–30.
5. Spicer, *46 Days of Christmas*, n.p.
6. Strich, *La Legende de Saint Nicholas*, n.p.
7. Thoennes, *Christmas in France*, 17.
8. Spicer, *46 Days*, n.p.
9. *Scribner's Magazine*, December, 1920.
10. Meriel Buchanan, 137–45.

BIBLIOGRAPHY

Ancelet-Hustache. *Saint Nicholas*. London: Cassell, 1960.

Armstrong, William. "A Christmas Visit to a Christmas Heart." New York: *The Delineator*, December 1917.

Barnes, Ian. *The Historical Atlas of the Bible*. Edison, NJ: Chartwell Books, Inc., 2006.

Beneduce, Ann Kay. *Joy to the World: A Family Christmas Treasury*. New York: Atheneum Books/Simon and Schuster, 2000.

Bennet, William J. *The True Saint Nicholas: Why He Matters to Christmas*. New York: Howard/Simon & Schuster, 2009.

Blair, Walter, Theodore Hornberger, and Randall Stewart. *The Literature of the United States*. Chicago: Scott Foresman and Company, 1949.

Bowler, Gerry. *Santa Claus: A Biography*. Toronto: McClelland & Stewart, 2005.

Brockett, Clyde W., et al. *The Saint Play in Medieval Europe*. Kalamazoo, MI: Medieval Institute Publications, 1986.

Cann, D. L. *Saint Nicholas: Bishop of Myra; The Life and Times of the Original Father Christmas*. Ottawa: Novalis, 2002.

Chaney, Elsa. *The Twelve Days of Christmas*. Collegeville, MN: Liturgical Press, 1986.

Chao, Jenifer. "Tis the Season for Old St. Nick. But the Dutch Wonder Which One?" Associated Press release, n.d.

The Church of St. Nicholas in Myra and Environs. Antalya, Turkey: Museum Publications, 1988.

Cioffari, P. Gerado, o.p. *Saint Nicholas: His Life, the Translation of His Relics and His Basilica in Bari*. Translated by Philip L. Barnes. Bari, Italy: Centro Studi Nicolaiani, 1994.

Coffin, Tristram Potter. *The Book of Christmas Folklore*. New York: Seabury Press, 1973.

Creasy, Sir Edward S. *The Fifteen Decisive Battles of the World*. New York: Heritage Press, 1969 (originally published in 1851).

Crichton, Robin. *Who Is Santa Claus: The True Story Behind a Living Legend*. Edinburgh, Scotland: Canongate Publishing, Ltd., 1987.

Culver, Virginia. "Epiphany Enjoys a Resurgence." Denver, *Denver Post*, Jan. 6, 2001.

Del Re, Gerald and Patricia. *The Christmas Almanac*. New York: Doubleday, 1979.

Durant, Will. The Story of Civilization series (*The Age of Faith*). New York: Simon & Schuster, 1950.

Eads, Richard. *The Confessions of St. Nicholas*. San Jose, CA: Writers Club Press, 1999.

Ebon, Martin. *Saint Nicholas: Life and Legend*. New York: Harper & Row, 1975.

Eich, John L. "How Does Santa Claus Fit with Christmas?" Northwestern Lutheran Magazine Web site, March 2, 2001.

Encyclopedia Britannica. 1946 ed., Chicago.

Englemann, Dennis E. *The Saint Nicholas Secret: A Story*

of Childhood Faith Reborn in the Heart of a Father. Ben
  Lomond, CA: Conciliar Press, 1999.

Fournier, Catherine and Peter. "Advent, Christmas and
  Epiphany in the Domestic Church." Waba, ON: Domestic
  Church Communication, Ltd. Web site, 2000.

From St. Nicolas to Santa Claus. Antalya, Turkey: Santa Claus
  Foundation, 1999.

Gibbons, Gail. *Santa Who?* New York: William Morrow
  Books, 1999.

Hadfield, Miles and John. *The Twelve Days of Christmas*.
  Boston: Little, Brown and Company, 1962.

Hargrove, Thomas, and Tom Hodges. "Americans Are Still Big
  Fans of St. Nick," *Chicago Sun Times*, 2000.

Hastings, Chris, and Danielle Demetriou. "Father Christmas Is
  Heading for the Sack in Britain." Dec. 18, 2000 news release.

Highfield, Roger. *Can Reindeer Fly?* London: Metro Books, 1998.

Horner, Jerri. "The Days of the Belsnickel," *Early American
  Life*. Christmas 1993.

Impink, Anne Stewart. "Translated Customs of the Pennsylvania
  Dutch," *Historical Review of Berks County* (winter 1969–1970).

Janson, H. W. *History of Art*. Englewood Cliffs, NJ: Prentice-
  Hall/Harry N. Abrams, 1977.

Jones, Charles W. *St. Nicholas of Myra, Bari, and Manhattan:
  Biography of a Legend*. Chicago: University of Chicago
  Press, 1978.

Kirkpatrick, David D. "Whose Jolly Old Elf Is That,
  Anyway?" *New York Times*, Oct. 26, 2000.

Kismaric, Carole and Felix. *A Gift from Saint Nicholas*. New York: Holiday House, 1988.

LeMoy, *L'Anjou* (Paris, 1924).

Lewis, C. S. *Mere Christianity*. New York: Collier Books/Macmillan Publishing Company, 1960.

Luckhardt, Mildred C. *The Story of Saint Nicholas*. New York: Abingdon Press, 1960.

Macdonald Palangi, Paula. "The Last Straw," in Joe Wheeler's *Christmas in My Heart 2*. Hagerstown, MD: Review and Herald Publishing, 1993.

Marquis, Bernie and Theresa Myers. *How St. Nicholas Became Santa Claus: The True Story*. Boston: Pauline Books & Media, 1993.

Markou, Antonios. *Concerning the Relics of St. Nicholas, Archbishop of Myra*. Etna, CA: Center for Traditionalist Orthodox Studies, 1994.

Mazar, Peter. *School Year, Church Year: Customs and Decorations for the Classroom*. Chicago, Liturgy Training Publications, 2001.

_____. *Winter: Celebrating the Season in a Christian Home*. Chicago: Liturgy Training Publications, 1996.

McKnight, George Harley. *St. Nicholas: His Legend and His Role in the Christmas Celebration and Other Popular Customs*. Gansevoort, NY: Corner House Historical Publications, 1917, 1996.

Miller, Llewellyn. "Children and Santa Claus." New York: *Redbook*. December, 1960.

Miller, Madeleine S. and J. Lane. *Harper's Bible Dictionary*. New York: Harpers & Brothers, 1952.

Miller, Olive Beaupré. *Tales Told in Holland*. Chicago: The Book House for Children, 1926, 1954.

Moffatt, Laurie Norton. *Norman Rockwell: A Definitive Catalogue*. Stockbridge, MA: The Norman Rockwell Museum, 1986. (2 vols).

Moore, Clement C. *The Night Before Christmas*. Philadelphia: Porter & Coats, 1883.

Twas the Night Before Christmas: A Visit from St. Nicholas. Boston: Houghton Mifflin Company, 1912.

Neuberger, Anne E. *St. Nicholas: The Wonder Worker*. Huntington, IN: Our Sunday Visitor Publishing Division, 2000.

Newland, Mary Reed. *The Saint Book*. New York: Seabury Press, 1979.

Nissenbaum, Stephen. *The Battle for Christmas*. New York: Vintage/Random House, 1996.

Pertwee, Jon and James Coco. "The Curious Case of Santa Claus." *Skyline Video* RELV 033, 1996.

Ramsey, Michael. Archbishop of Canterbury's Ascension Eve 1956 sermon.

Reed, Walt and Roger. *The Illustrator in America: 1800–1980*. New York: Madison Square Press, 1984.

Remson, Al. *Christmas: A Celebration in Song and Story*. New York: Berkley/Perigee, 1999.

Robbins, Maria, and Jim Charlton. *A Christmas Companion*. New York: Putnam/Perigee, 1989.

Roberts, David. "He's the Word Sleuth." *Reader's Digest*, April 2002.

Rosenthal, James. "Celebrating Christian Style." London: *Anglican World* St. Nicholas special, Christmas 2001.

_____. "Come Home, Santa, All Is Forgiven." London: *Church Times*, Dec. 24, 31, 1999.

_____. "St. Nicholas, a Necessary Tradition." London: *Anglican World*, December 2000.

_____. "Who Was Saint Nicholas?" London: *Anglican World*, St. Nicholas Special, Christmas 2000.

Runcie, Lord (former archbishop of Canterbury). "In Quest of Father Christmas." London: *Anglican World*, Christmas 2002 special.

"Santa Claus: The Dutch Way—The Birth of Santa Claus," n.p., n.d.

"Santa Claus, Saint Nicholas, and the Mystery of Christmas." *The Catholic Commentator*. Dec. 16, 1998.

Seal, Jeremy. *Nicholas: The Epic Journey from Saint to Santa Claus*. New York: Bloomberry, 2005.

Serwer, Andy. "The Decade from Hell." New York: *Time*, Dec. 7, 2009.

Shephard, Aaron. *The Baker's Dozen: A Saint Nicholas Tale*. New York: Simon & Schuster, 1995.

Simons, Marlise. "Sorry Old St. Nick: These Days, Dutch Santa Takes Abuse, Even from His U. S. Offspring." New York Times News Service, 1996.

Spicer, Dorothy Gladys. *46 Days of Christmas*. New York: Coward, McCann & Geoghegan, 1960.

Stiegermeyer, Julien. *Saint Nicholas: The Real Story of the Christmas Legend*. St. Louis: Concordia Publishing House, 2003.

Stredder, Eleanor. "The Twelfth Cake and Its Story." *Little Folks*. 1875.

Strich, Marie-José. *La Legende de Saint Nicholas*. Rennes, France: Editions Oueste-France, 1998.

Suk, L'Tishia. "Celebrate Advent!" *Focus on the Family Magazine*, December 2000.

Thoennes, Kristin. *Christmas in France*. New York: Grolier/Hilltop, 1999.

Tompert, Ann. *Saint Nicholas*. Honesday, PA: Boyds Mill Press, 2000.

2000–2009: The Decade That Changed the World. New York: Life Books, 2009.

Vaughan, Bill. "Tell Me a Story of Christmas," in Joe Wheeler's *Christmas in My Heart 2*. Hagerstown, MD: Review and Herald Publishing, 1993.

Veggie Tales, *Saint Nicholas: A Story of Joyful Giving*. Big Ideas DVD, 2009.

Walwin, Peggy. *St. Nicholas: Our Santa Claus*. Gloucester, England: Albert E. Smith, Printers Ltd., 1971.

West, Matthew. *Give This Christmas Away*. Carol Stream, IL: Tyndale House, 2009.

Wheeler, Joe. "From St. Nicholas to Santa Claus," Introduction for *Christmas in My Heart 6*. Hagerstown, MD: Review and Herald Publishing, 1997; also in *Christmas in My Soul 2*. Doubleday/Random House, 2000.

_____. "Hans and the Trading Game," in *Christmas in My Heart 5*, Hagerstown, MD: Review and Herald Publishing, 1996.

_____. "A Pennsylvania Deutsch Christmas," Introduction for *Christmas in My Heart 4*. Hagerstown, MD, Review and Herald Publishing, 1995.

_____. "Scrooge at the Crossroads," Introduction for Dickens's *The Christmas Carol*. Wheaton, IL: Tyndale House Publishers/Focus on the Family, 1997.

_____. "The 36 Days of Christmas," Introduction for *Christmas in My Heart, Second Treasury*. New York: Doubleday, 1997.

Wheeler, Joe, and James Rosenthal. *St. Nicholas: A Closer Look at Christmas*. Nashville: Thomas Nelson, 2005.

Whelan, Gloria. *The Miracle of Saint Nicholas*. San Francisco: Bethlehem Books/Ignatius Press, 1997.

Willis, Lloyd A., Ph.D. (Professor of Archeology and Biblical History, Southwestern Adventist University). Interview by Joe Wheeler. Keene, TX, 22 June 2002.

Yzermans, Vincent A. *Wonderworker: The True Story of How St. Nicholas Became Santa Claus*. Chicago: Acta Publications, 1994.

ABOUT THE AUTHOR

Joe Wheeler, PhD, is considered to be one of America's leading anthologizers of stories, and has written or edited seventy-one books, including the Great Stories Remembered series, the Heart to Heart series, and the best-selling Christmas in My Heart series. He is emeritus professor of English at Washington Adventist University in Takoma Park, Maryland; cofounder and executive director of the Zane Grey's West Society; and general editor at Focus on the Family. Dr. Wheeler and his wife, Connie, currently reside in Conifer, Colorado.

www.joewheelerbooks.com

Close Encounters of the Christian Kind

Available Now

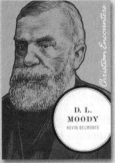

D.L. MOODY
9781595550477

SERGEANT YORK
9781595550255

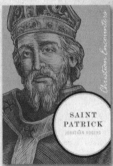

SAINT PATRICK
9781595553058

JANE AUSTEN (9781595553027)
ANNE BRADSTREET (9781595551092)
WILLIAM F. BUCKLEY (9781595550651)
WINSTON CHURCHILL (9781595550477)

ISAAC NEWTON (9781595553034)
SAINT FRANCIS (9781595551078)
JOHN BUNYAN (9781595553041)

Available April 2011

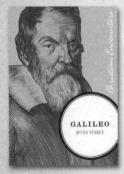

GALILEO
9781595550316

ALBERT SCHWEITZER
9781595550798

JOHANN SEBASTIAN BACH
9781595551085